50-

AF800070

USER'S HANDBOOK TO THE IBM PERSONAL COMPUTER®

User's Handbook To The IBM Personal Computer®

by Jeffrey R. Weber

Weber Systems Inc.
Cleveland, Ohio

IBM Personal Computer® is a registered trademark of International Business Machines Corporation.

Published by
Weber Systems Inc.
8437 Mayfield Road
Cleveland, Ohio 44026
USA

For information on translations and distributors outside the USA, please write Weber Systems Inc. at the above address.

User's Handbook to the IBM Personal Computer

LC 82-071681
ISBN 0-938862-13-8

Disclaimer of Warranties and Limitation or Liability

The authors have taken due care in preparing this book and the programs contained in it. The authors and Weber Systems Inc. make no express or implied warranty of any kind regarding these programs or their documentation in this book. In no event shall Weber Systems Inc. or the authors be liable for incidental or consequential damages in connection with or arising out of the furnishing, performance, or use of this book.

Layout Design: Shelly Harpold
Cover Design & Illustrations: Anne Cornell

CONTENTS

Chapter 1. Introduction To The IBM PC

Overview

The introduction of the Personal Computer by IBM caused a revolution in the microcomputer industry. The IBM Personal Computer is called by many the best microcomputer yet brought to market.

In an industry previously dominated by Apple Computer, Commodore International, and Tandy, IBM is creating a competitive stir. IBM microcomputer sales are estimated to grow from $360 million in 1982 to $2.3 billion in 1986. The retail value of IBM software sold is estimated to grow from $85 million in 1982 to $700 million in 1986. The value of PC hardware related items made by other companies is estimated to grow from $65 million in 1982 to $685 million in 1986. The value of software related sales made by other firms is estimated to grow from $15 million in 1982 to $395 million in 1986.

The total for all of the above categories should exceed $4 billion by 1986. In short, IBM will create a $4 billion industry with its Personal Computer.

The basic IBM Personal Computer consists of two separate units; the **Keyboard** and the **System Unit.** These are shown in Illustration 1-1.

The Keyboard Unit consists of a main keyboard with a standard typewriter style keyboard layout. To the left of the main keyboard is a numeric keypad. To the right of the main keyboard is a set of 10 function keys. A total of 83 keys are contained on the Keyboard Unit.

The Keyboard Unit is connected to the System Unit via a coiled cable. The System Unit contains the heart of the PC -- an Intel 8088 microprocessor, up to 64K of **dynamic RAM** (random access memory), the 40K extended Microsoft BASIC in **ROM** (read-only memory), up to two disk drives, a cassette interface, a built-in speaker, and five expansion slots. Additional **dynamic** RAM memory cards can be placed into the expansion slots to bring the total amount of RAM to 256K.

Additional peripherals can be purchased to round out your basic IBM PC into a total microcomputer system. These include the IBM Monochrome Display, which is the video display terminal for the system, and the IBM 80 CPS Matrix Printer. (The 80 CPS stands for 80 characters per second -- the printer's speed.) These items are pictured in Illustration 1-1.

Illustration 1-1 IBM PC System Unit & Keyboard

Table 1-1. IBM PC System Components

Component		Description
System Unit	Size:	width 20 inches, depth 16 inches, height 5.5 inches; weight (without drives) 21 pounds, weight (with 2 disk drives) 28 pounds
	Power:	120 VAC
	Processor:	Intel 8088
	Standard Features:	Keyboard Unit & cable cassette recorder connector, five expansion slots, BASIC interpreter, 16K RAM.
Disk Drives		Up to two 5-inch floppy disk drives. 160K each.
Operating System		IBM PC DOS (Microsoft)
Optional Hardware		Monochrome Video Display
		Combination Monochrome Display Adapter & Printer Adapter
		Color Graphics Monitor Adapter
		16K RAM expansion
		32K RAM expansion
		64K RAM expansion
		Disk Drive Adapter
		Disk Drive (5-inch Floppy disks)

Table 1-1. IBM PC System Components (Cont.)

Component	Description
	Asynchronous Communications Adapter
	Game Control Adapter
	Printer
	Printer Adapter
	Printer Cable
	Printer Stand
Available Software (2/1/82)	BASIC Interpreter (Microsoft) standard
	Extended BASIC Interpreter (Microsoft)
	PASCAL Compiler (Microsoft)
	Visicalc (Personal Software)
	Peachtree Accounting System
	Adventure (Microsoft)
	Advanced Diagnostics Package

System Board

The System Board, or motherboard, is the main circuit board of a micromputer system. Most of the circuitry for the PC is placed on its System Board including:

Microprocessor(s)	Expansion Slots
ROM Memory	Cassette Interface
RAM Memory	Keyboard Interface
DMA Circuits	Speaker & Timing Circuits

Illustration 1-2. IBM System Board

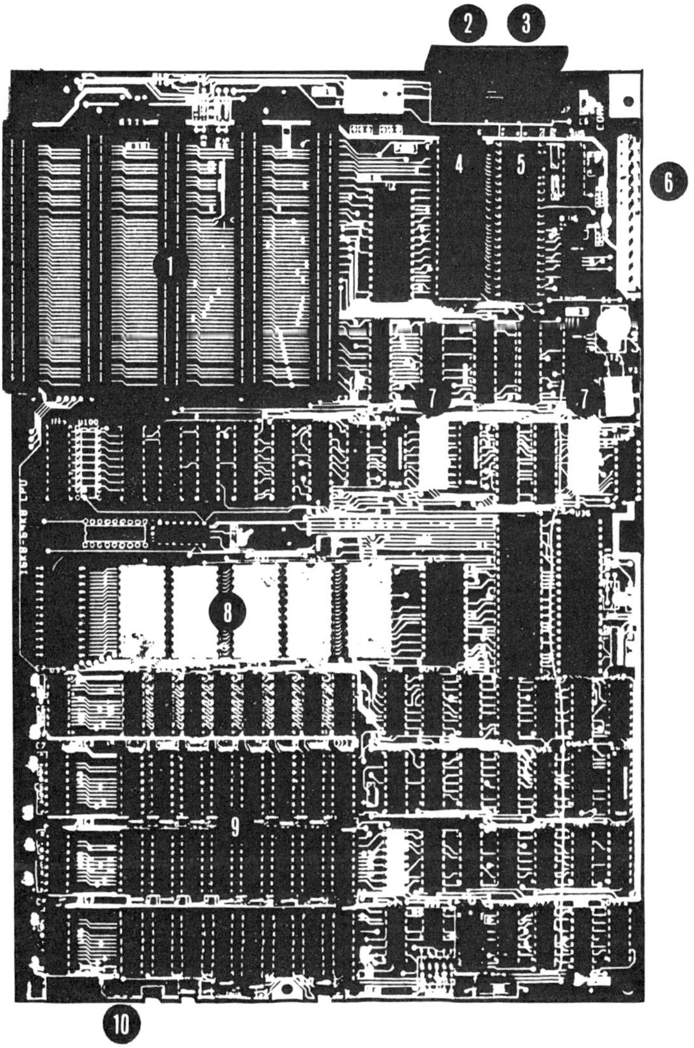

1 -- Expansion slots
2 -- Cassette connection
3 -- Keyboard unit connection
4 -- Intel 8088 CPU
5 -- 8087 co-processor socket
6 -- Power supply connection
7 -- DIP switches
8 -- ROM chips
9 -- RAM chips
10 -- Speaker connection

ROM and RAM

ROM stands for Read-Only Memory. ROM will hold the data stored in it permanently. If the power to the PC is shut off, the information stored in ROM will remain there. As previously mentioned, the Microsoft BASIC language interpreter is stored in ROM.

RAM stands for Random Access Memory*. Any data stored in RAM is lost when the PC's power is shut off. When data is loaded from a tape cassette, a disk drive, or the keyboard, it is stored in RAM.

Dynamic and Static RAM

There are two different types of RAM memory; **dynamic RAM** and **static RAM**. Dynamic RAM can only hold the data it is storing for a few milliseconds. Therefore, any data being stored in dynamic RAM must constantly be rewritten or refreshed. This dynamic RAM refresh function must be a part of the support logic when the dynamic RAM memory is designed.

Static RAM is more expensive than dynamic RAM. However, once data has been written into static RAM, it will be retained as long as power is supplied. A description of the ROM and RAM used in the IBM PC is given in Tables 1-2 and 1-3 respectively.

IBM ROM

As mentioned in the previous section, ROM is a type of memory that will hold the data stored in it permanently. The IBM PC uses ROM to store programs that are essential to the operation of the computer.

These programs being stored in ROM are often called **firmware** (software in hardware). The IBM PC uses ROM to store its **BIOS, BASIC interpreter,** and **bootstrap loader.**

The bootstrap loader is a start-up program that starts the disk drive and then loads the computer's operating system from the system diskette.

*Random Access Memory is a somewhat misleading term to describe RAM, as most memory (including ROM) is randomly accessed.

The IBM PC's ROM is contained on the System Board. Although the System Board has the capability of holding six 8K ROM chips, only five of the six sockets are currently utilized. IBM may be planning to use the sixth socket for a future enchancement to the PC.

In addition to the 64K of ROM possible on the System Board, an additional 192K is available for use by placing ROM expansion cards in the expansion slots. This additional ROM capacity might be used at some future date for placing applications software on ROM or including additional BIOS routines for adding new peripherals to the PC.

Table 1-2. IBM ROM (Read-Only Memory)

IBM ROM Capacity	
Manufacturer:	Motorola
Total Capacity	256K (48K Capacity on System Board)
Currently Used:	40K on System Board 5-8K ROM's
Programs in ROM:	BIOS BASIC Intepreter

IBM RAM

As previously mentioned, RAM is a type of memory meant for temporary storage of data.

The IBM PC comes equipped with 16K of RAM on its System Board. An additional 48K of RAM may be added to the System Board. The first 16K of RAM is wired into place on the System Board, while the additional 48K are placed in sockets, so as to allow non-technicians to easily expand the computer's RAM capacity.

Each 16K of RAM on the System Board consists of 9 chips, each with a 2K capacity. On the surface, it appears as if this is one chip too many.

However, the IBM PC uses the ninth memory chip to perform **parity checks** on the other RAM chips. Parity checks are constant tests conducted on the RAM in which the number of individual bits which are "on" is added and rechecked to be certain no data has been lost. If the RAM should fail a parity check test, the following message will appear on the screen:

PARITY ERROR

and the program currently being run will be aborted.

In addition to the System Board's 64K RAM capacity, an additional 192K of RAM can be added to the PC by adding RAM expansion cards into the expansion slots inside the PC System Unit. IBM distributes 32K and 64K RAM expansion cards for this purpose.

Table 1-3. IBM RAM (Random Access Memory)

IBM RAM Capacity	
RAM Type:	4116 type; 2K each 250 nanosecond access time 450 nanosecond cycle time
Row Configuration:	16K per row; 9 chips per row (9th chip used for parity checking)
Board Configuration:	System Board -- 4 rows (1 row soldered, remainder placed in sockets) 32K Expansion Board -- 2 rows 64K Expansion Board -- 4 rows
RAM Capacity:	System Board--16K (standard) System Board--48K (possible expansion) Expansion Slots -- 192K (additional) Possible Future Expansion -- 384K
RAM Characteristics:	Dynamic RAM usable with Direct Memory Addressing (DMA)

The PC's 8088 microprocessor allows up to 1 **megabyte** (one million bytes) of addressable memory. Of that 1 megabyte, 128K is utilized by the PC for the Graphics and Display Adapter, 256K is utilized for ROM, and 640K are utilized for RAM. Therefore, space exists for an additional 384K of RAM. This may be a future development on the part of IBM.

IBM BIOS

BIOS is an abbreviation for the term BASIC Input/Output System. The BIOS is a collection of programs that control the transfer of characters between the microprocessor and the various devices connected to it (i.e. printer, video display, keyboard, communications adapter, etc.).

The PC's BIOS also contains the cassette tape operating system, a power-on self-test, the graphics character generator, the System Configuration analysis program (which gives the memory size and peripherals used), a time of day clock, and a mini-floppy disk drive bootstrap loader.

Microcomputers designed around 8 bit microprocessors tend to limit the number and size of programs stored in BIOS because the 8 bit microprocessor can address only a fraction of the memory that a 16 bit processor can. The PC with its 16 bit microprocessor and its ability to address up to 1 MB allows for the more extensive use of ROM.

One advantage to placing the BIOS in ROM is that its programs are available when the computer is turned on. However, placing BIOS in ROM also presents some difficulties, in that the BIOS routines may not be changed to allow for the addition of new devices.

IBM has provided for the addition of devices to its ROM based BIOS, without actually changing the ROM chips, by reserving several Interrupt Vectors. Even so, it may eventually be necessary to replace the ROM chips currently used in the PC's System Board, if the BIOS is to be changed substantially.

Table 1-4. IBM BIOS (BASIC Input/Output System) Features

IBM BIOS	
Purpose:	BIOS controls the transfer of data between the microprocessor and various system devices (i.e. keyboard, video display, printer, communications card, etc.).
Designed By:	Microsoft Inc.
Location:	8K ROM Chip contained on System Board
Programs:	1. Cassette Operating System 2. Power-On Self-Test 3. I/O routines for video display, keyboard, printer, and communications adapter 4. Graphics Character Generator 5. System Configuration Analysis (memory size, peripherals used) 6. Time-of-Day Clock 7. Mini-Floppy Disk Drive Bootstrap Loader

Table 1-5. IBM BIOS Interrupt Vectors

Interrupt Number		Name	BIOS Initialization
0		Divide by Zero	None
1		Single Step	None
2		Non Maskable	NMI_INT (F000:E2C3)
3		Breakpoint	None
4		Overflow	None
5		Print Screen	PRINT_SCREEN (F000:FF54)
6		Unused	
7		Unused	
8	8259 Interrupt Vectors	Time of Day	TIMER_INT(F000:FEA5)
9		Keyboard	KB_INT (F000:E987)
A		Unused	
B		Unused	
C		Unused (Reserved Communications)	
D		Unused	
E		Diskette	DISK_INT (F000:EF57)
F		Unused (Reserved Printer)	
10	BIOS Entry Points	Video	VIDEO_I O (F000:F065)
11		Equipment Check	EQUIPMENT (F000:F84D)
12		Memory	MEMORY_SIZE_DETERMINE (F000:F8411)
13		Diskette	DISKETTE_I O (F000:EC59)
14		Communications	RS232__I O (F000:E739)
15		Cassette	CASSETTE__I O (F000:F859)
16		Keyboard	KEYBOARD_ I O (F000:E82E)
17		Printer	PRINTER_I O (F000:EF02)
18		Cassette BASIC	(F600:0000)
19		Bootstrap	BOOT_STRAP (F000:E6F2)
1A		Time of Day	TIME_OF_DAY (F000:FEGE)
1B		Keyboard Break	DUMMY_RETURN (F000:FF53)
1C		Timer Tick	DUMMY_RETURN (F000:FF53)
1D		Video Initialization	VIDEO_PARMS (F000:F0A4)
1E		Diskette Parameters	DISK_BASE (F000:EFC7)
1F		Video Graphics Chars	None

IBM's CPU

The central processing unit or **CPU** is the heart of any computer. The CPU controls all of the other components for the computer.

In larger computers, the CPU and the **ALU** (Arithmetic logic unit) consist of a group of IC chips each dedicated to its own task. In smaller computers, the CPU and ALU are generally combined on a single chip, which is known as a **microprocessor**.

A microprocessor can be defined as a single chip which contains the logic of a central processing unit as well as any additional logic that must complement the CPU.

The microprocessor used in the PC is the Intel 8088, which is manufactured by Intel Corporation of Sunnyvale, California. Intel is a pioneer in the development of microprocessors. Intel developed the predecessor of the 8088, the 4004 calculator chip, in the early 1970's. Intel subsequently developed the 8008, 8080, 8085, and 8088/8086 microprocessors. The difference between the 8088 and 8086 will be discussed shortly.

Microprocessor logic is based upon the **bit**. A bit is the basis of all information storage within the computer. A bit consists of a simple switch that can consist of either of the two binary states, on or off.

Bits are often separated into groups of eight. These groups of 8 bits are known as a **byte**. A byte is required to represent a single character (i.e. letter, number, or symbol). Generally, bytes are processed by the computer in groups of 2.

Most of the 8-bit microprocessors can only **address** (or work directly with) 65,535 (64K) bytes at any one time. Even though this number appears large, a 30 page document would fill this memory area.

Most 16-bit microprocessors can address from 256,000 to 16 million bytes of memory. Moreover, 16 bit microprocessors process data at a speed from 2 to 10 times faster than 8-bit microprocessors.

Illustration 1-3. Close-Up of Intel 8088 Chip

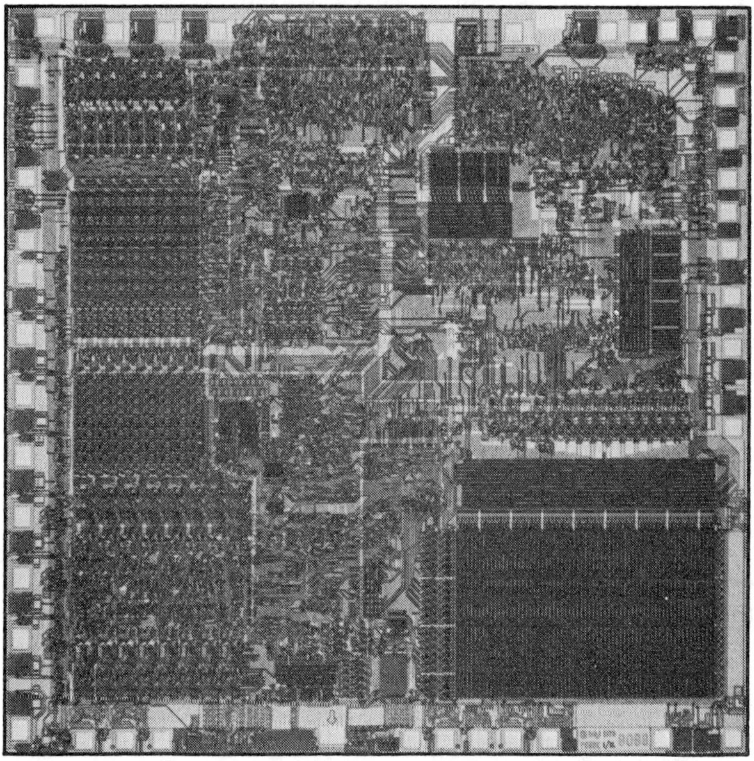

Courtesy: Intel Corporation

Intel 8088 CPU

One of the main advantages the IBM PC has over other microcomputers is the power provided by its use of the 8088 CPU.

The 8088 can address up to one million bytes of memory (or 1 megabyte, abbreviated as 1MB). The 8088 has 20 different address lines, which allows 2 to exponent 20 (2^{20}) different address combinations. This is the equivalent of 1,048,576 different addresses.

The speed of the 8088 is about .65 mps (or million operations per second). In other words, the 8088 will process 650,000 arithmetic operations or data transfers per second. When compared with the Intel 8080A, the 8088 is approximately six times faster.

The characteristics of the 8088 are outlined in Table 1-6.

Intel 8087 Numeric Data Processor

Most CPU's perform mathematic operations relatively slowly--especially when non-integer numbers are involved. This is due to the fact that with non-integer numbers, the microprocessor must be given instructions on how to perform math calculations.

To speed the processing of math operations, many mini and main-frame computers use a separate processor to perform numeric operations. These are known as math processors or floating point co-processors.

A math processor contains the internal logic needed to perform math operations internally, rather than relying on an external set of program constructions. Math processors can outperform CPU's by a factor of as much as 100 to 1.

The Intel 8087 Numeric Data Processor is the math co-processor for the Intel 8086 and 8088 CPU's. Full-scale production of the 8087 is expected in the middle of 1982.

The System Board for the IBM PC contains a 40-pin socket which is named the Aux Processor Socket. The circuit lines running to this empty socket are for the eventual addition of the Intel 8087 math co-processor.

Table 1-6. Intel 8088 Characteristics

Intel 8088	
Construction:	Chip technology -- HMOS 40 pin plastic package
Manufacturer:	Intel Corporation
Introduction Date:	1979
Features:	1. 20 address lines 2. 1 MB memory addressing 3. 650,000 operations per second 4. 8 data lines 5. 4.77 Mhz clock speed 6. Separate bus interface and execution units 7. 99 basic machine language instructions 8. Software compatible with Intel 8086

It is expected that when the 8087 is available for use with the IBM PC, the PC will experience an increase in numeric processing speed by a factor of at least 20.

The characteristics of the Intel 8087 are given in Table 1-7.

Microsoft BASIC Interpreter

Microsoft BASIC is the version of BASIC that is standard with the IBM PC. The BASIC **interpreter** (explained on page 38) is contained in 40K of ROM. The various features of Microsoft BASIC will be discussed in detail in Chapters 8 and 9. Our discussion here is merely meant to be an introduction.

Table 1-7. Intel 8087 Characteristics

Intel 8087 Numeric Data Processor	
Manufacturer:	Intel Corporation
Introduction Date:	1980
Characteristics:	1. Includes built-in math instructions for addition, subtraction, multiplication, division, square root, absolute value, tangent, arctangent and others. 2. Handles integers up to 18 digits in length and floating point numbers 16 to 80 bits wide. 3. Compatible with Intel 8086/8088 microprocessors.

The IBM PC uses three separate versions of BASIC; Cassette BASIC, Disk BASIC and Advanced BASIC.

Cassette BASIC is the version of BASIC used when a cassette recorder is being used to store information. Cassette BASIC can not be used when data is being stored on diskettes.

Disk BASIC contains all of the capabilities of Cassette BASIC and can also be used when data is being stored on diskettes. In other words, Disk BASIC can be used when data is being stored on diskettes or when it is being stored on cassette tape.

Advanced BASIC has all of the capabilities of Cassette BASIC and Disk BASIC as well as additional features not found on these other two versions of BASIC. Advanced BASIC includes several graphics commands such as CIRCLE, DRAW, and PAINT that allow the user to fully utilize the graphics capabilities of the IBM PC when it is equipped with the Color/Graphics Monitor Adapter and a color monitor or color TV set.

Both the Advanced BASIC and the Disk BASIC versions require DOS before they can be run, or before any programs written in Advanced or Disk BASIC can be run. DOS is required to manage the input and output from your disk units.

IBM PC Peripherals

In the remaining sections of Chapter 1, we will discuss some of the peripheral components that can be added to your IBM PC. These include the following:

Disk Drives
Monochrome Display
IBM 80 CPS Printer
Monochrome Display/Printer Adapter Card
Color/Graphics Monitor Adapter Card
Color Monitors
Asynchronous Communications Adapter

Disk Drives and DOS

The optional disk drives for the IBM PC are **soft sectored, double density, single sided** drives. The floppy disk drives use 40 tracks per disk with eight 512 byte **sectors** per track. This gives a total of 163,840 bytes of data storage per drive.

The IBM Disk Operating System (DOS) is a group of programs that allow the user to manipulate information between the diskette drives, memory, and the video screen.

Disk Drives Explained

The disk drive is one of the most important parts of a computer system. Disk drives allow the storage of large amounts of data. An IBM 5¼ inch disk can store 163,840 characters of data. This is approximately three and one half times as much data as can be stored on 48K of RAM.

Unlike RAM storage, when information is stored on a disk, the information is not lost when the computer is turned off. In other words, disks offer a permanent means of storing data.

A disk stores data in a magnetic form, much like data is stored on magnetic tape. The main difference between storage on a magnetic tape and storage on a disk is that the disk surface is round--much like a record's surface.

The disk drive contains a device known as a **read/write head**, which is used to read and write information. The computer can move the head to any position desired on the disk surface. This is in contrast to magnetic tape, where data is read from or written onto the tape in consecutive order.

This capacity to read or write data at a particular position is known as **random access.** Disk drives are known as random access storage devices. On the other hand, in cases where data must be read or written in a consecutive order, the accessing is known as **sequential access**. A cassette tape recorder is known as a sequential access device.

Types of Disks

There are three primary types of disks used by microcomputers; **hard disks, Winchester disks,** and **floppy diskettes.** These will be described in the following sections.

Currently, IBM offers floppy diskette storage for the IBM Personal Computer. However, it is expected that IBM will also offer Winchester or hard disk storage in the near future.

Hard Disks

Microcomputer hard disk systems generally allow storage of 5 to 30 megabytes of data. One megabyte is the equivalent of one million bytes. The hard disk itself is made of a rigid material with a magnetic coating. The disk drive and the hard disk are separate units. The operator can remove one hard disk and replace it with another.

Table 1-8. IBM Disk Drives

IBM Disk Drives	
Purpose:	Provides storage for program and data files.
Manufacturer:	Tandon Magnetics Inc.
Capacity:	Single-sided/double-density (SSDD); rated for quad density. Unformatted -- 250K currently; potential of 500K. Formatted -- 160K (when using PC DOS). 48 tracks per inch -- 40 tracks used 8 sectors per track 512 bytes per sector
Speed:	8 ms. seek time (track to track) 25 ms. head setting time 500 ms. maximum start/stop time 250,000 bits/second transfer rate

Winchester Disk Drives

Winchester disk drives are designed so that from 6 to 10 times more data can be stored on their surface than on a standard floppy diskette. Winchester disks must be kept very clean as they are extremely vulnerable to dust, dirt and smoke.

Since they must be kept so clean, Winchester disks must be sealed inside of the disk drive. This means that Winchester disks cannot be changed.

Since Winchester disks cannot be removed, floppy disk systems often are used in conjunction with Winchester disks to allow for back-up storage. Winchester disk systems are generally used with microcomputers rather than hard disk systems. A Winchester drive is shown in Illustration 1-4.

Illustration 1-4. Winchester Disk System

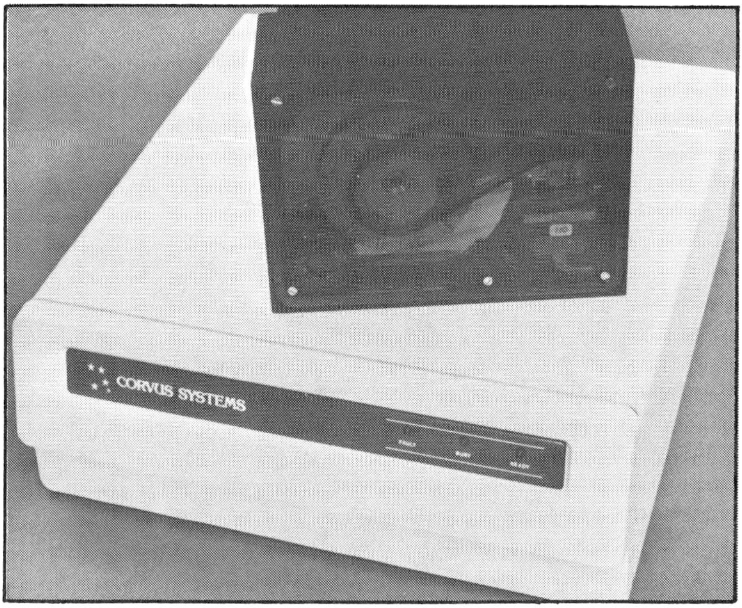

Courtesy: Corvus Systems, Inc.

Floppy Diskettes

The most widely used type of disk storage with microcomputers is floppy disk storage. A floppy diskette consists of a round vinyl disk which is enclosed within a plastic cover. The diskette is generally stored in a diskette envelope.

This cover protects the diskette from damage while it is being handled by the operator. The diskette should never be removed from its cover. A 5¼ inch diskette with its protective envelope is shown in Illustration 1-5.

The diskette is allowed to rotate within the protective envelope.

The round hole in the middle of the diskette allows the disk drive to hold the diskette and spin it. The oblong shaped opening on the protective envelope provides an area where the head can read from or write to the diskette surface.

Illustration 1-5. Mini-Floppy Diskette

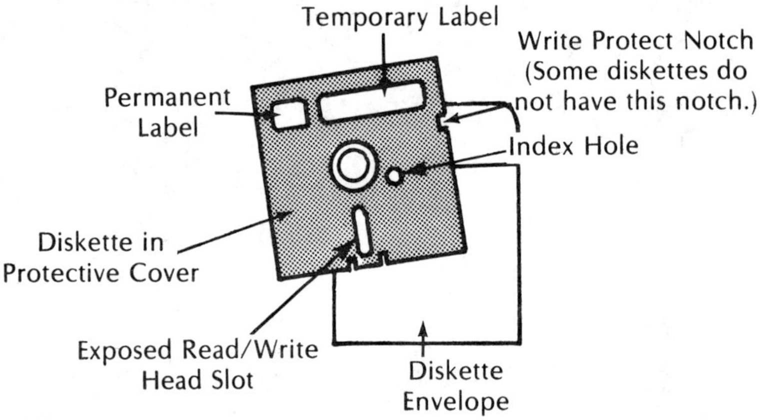

Floppy diskettes come in two sizes: 8 inch and 5¼ inch. The 5¼ inch diskettes are also known as mini-floppy diskettes. The IBM Personal Computer uses mini-floppy diskettes.

Tracks & Sectors

To facilitate the process of searching for data on the diskette surface, that surface is divided into tracks and sectors.

Tracks may be visualized as a series of concentric circles on the diskette surface, as shown in Illustration 1-6. IBM's DOS divides a diskette into 40 tracks.

To further reduce the time necessary to search for a particular data item, IBM's DOS divides each track into 8 sectors, which are also shown in Illustration 1-6.

Illustration 1-6. Tracks and Sectors

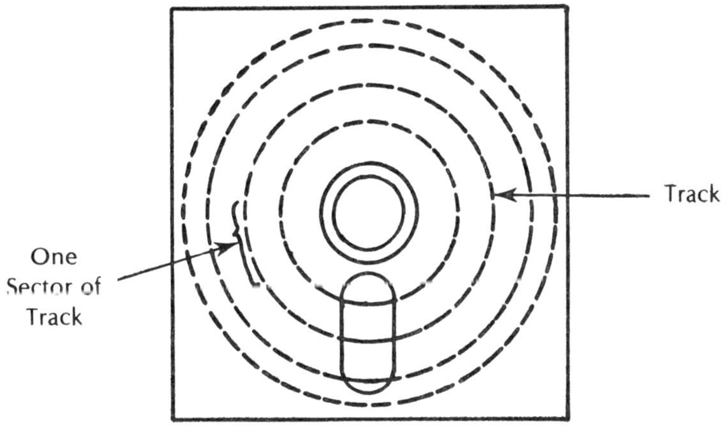

Each individual sector holds 512 bytes of data. When DOS has access to the track and sector where a particular data item is being stored, it will only have to search 512 bytes to find that item. The result of dividing the diskette surface into tracks and sectors is that access time is greatly decreased.

Hard and Soft Sectors

Locating a particular track on the disk surface is a relatively uncomplicated matter. The drive merely moves the head to the position on the diskette where the specified track is located, much like the needle on a phonograph is positioned to the location of a specific song on a record album.

However, locating a particular sector is a more difficult process. Two different methods are used to locate sectors on a disk; hard sectoring and soft sectoring.

Both the hard and soft sector methods involve the use of an index hole. The index hole is shown in Illustration 1-5. It is located just to the right of the large hole in the middle of the 5¼ inch diskette.

The index hole as shown in Illustration 1-5 is a hole only in the diskette's protective covering. Another index hole is located on the actual diskette surface inside the envelope. As the diskette spins, the index hole (or holes) on the diskette surface passes underneath the hole in the protective envelope.

A light source inside the disk drive shines light onto the area of the diskette containing the index hole. When an index hole on the disk surface is aligned with the index hole on the protective envelope, the light will shine through to a sensor. The sensor will relay information on the location of the index holes, which can be used to calculate the various sector locations.

Now that we have discussed the concepts of locating sectors, we will discuss the difference between hard and soft sectored diskettes. A hard sectored diskette contains a number of holes, each of which indicates the location of a sector. An extra hole is used to indicate the location of the first sector. The location of the various sectors is determined by counting the number of holes occuring after the first sector. A hard sectored diskette is depicted in Illustration 1-7.

Soft sectored diskettes have only one index hole as shown in Illustration 1-8. This solitary index hole marks the location of the first sector. By timing the rotation speed of the floppy diskette, the location of the other sectors can be determined. The IBM PC uses soft-sectored diskettes.

Illustration 1-7. Hard Sectored Diskette

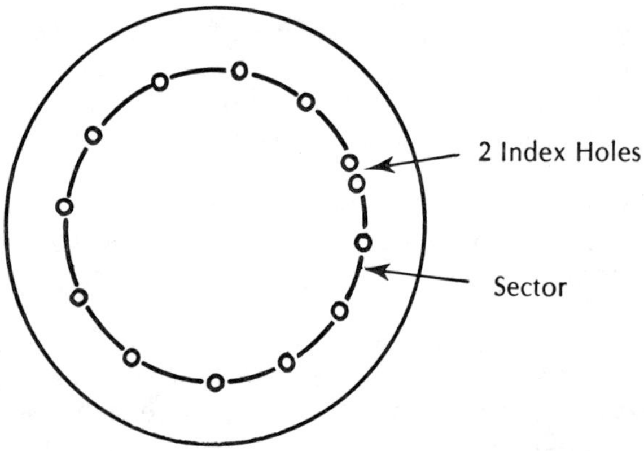

Illustration 1-8. Soft Sectored Diskette

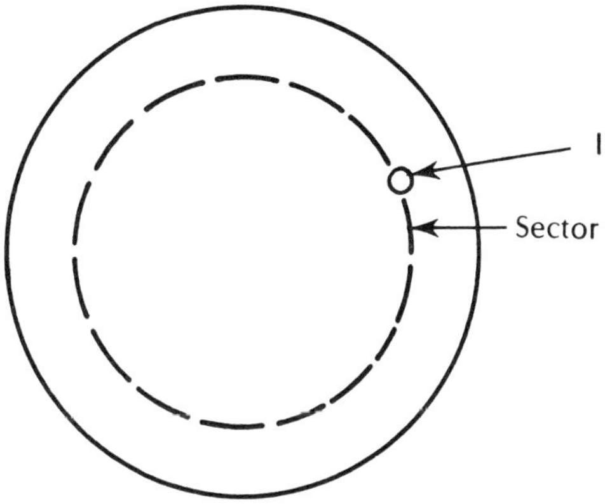

Single and Double Sided Diskettes

Some floppy diskettes are designed to be written on only one side. These are known as single sided (SS) diskettes.

Diskettes which are designed to be written on both sides are known as double sided (DS) diskettes.

Single, Double and Quad Density Diskettes

Density refers to a diskette's recording format, which in turn affects its capacity. Single density 5¼" diskettes have roughly 94K of capacity, double density 5¼" diskettes have a capacity of about 140-160K, and quad density 5¼" diskettes have a capacity of up to 370K.

The disk drives on the IBM PC use single sided double density diskettes, although they are rated for quad density. IBM's DOS currently limits each diskette's capacity to 160K.

Diskette Write Protection

Diskettes have a notch on the side of their protective envelope which determines whether or not data can be written onto that diskette. On 8 inch diskettes, this notch is known as a write-protect notch. On 5¼ inch diskettes, it is known as a write-enable notch.

On an 8 inch diskette, information cannot be written onto the diskette unless this notch has been covered. On 5¼ inch diskettes, information cannot be written onto the diskette unless the notch is left uncovered.

Some 5¼ inch diskettes (especially system diskettes) may be permanently write protected if their protective envelope does not contain a notch. Any 5¼ inch diskette with a notch can be write protected by merely covering the notch with a piece of tape as shown in Illustration 1-9.

Illustration 1-9. Write Protecting a 5¼ inch Diskette

Disk Operating Systems

The IBM offers not just one, but three different **operating systems,** PC DOS, UCSD p-System, and CP/M 86. Each of these three operating systems undertake similiar functions. However, the manner in which these functions are attained is quite different. The differences between these operating systems are very significant, and each in effect gives the PC a different personality.

An operating system can be defined as a group of programs which manage the computer's operation. A disk operating system can be defined as a group of programs that manage the transfer of data to and from a storage device such as disk or magnetic tape.

We will briefly discuss each of the currently available operating systems for the PC in the next three sections.

IBM DOS

IBM's DOS was written by Seattle Computer Products in 1980. Later, Microsoft Inc. acquired the exclusive marketing rights to this system. Microsoft then renamed the system as MS DOS. Subsequently, Lifeboat Associates began distributing the MS DOS system under the name SB-86. IBM uses the MS DOS system under the name PC DOS.

PC DOS, MS DOS, and SB-86 are the same disk operating systems. For our purposes, we will refer to this system as PC DOS.

In some ways, DOS resembles CP/M, a disk operating system marketed by Digital Research. For example, IBM's DOS uses the same system prompt (A>) as does CP/M.

However, in actuality, IBM's DOS is a version of Microsoft's Xenix operating system. Xenix is in turn a version of the Unix operating system which was originally developed by Western Electric.

CP/M-86

Digital Research's CP/M, with over 400,000 registered users, is the most widely used operating system for 8 bit microcomputers. Whether or not CP/M-86 will be maintained as a standard for 16 bit microcomputers remains to be seen.

CP/M-80 (8 bit version) is currently available on Zenith, Intertec, DEC, Wang, Xerox, and Lanier microcomputers as well as selected microcomputers manufactured by the industry leaders, Apple and Tandy.

CP/M was developed by Dr. Gary Kildall while he was an engineer at Intel Corporation. Intel had recently developed the 8008 microprocessor. Dr. Kildall and his associates had written a high level compiler known as PL/M to work with the chip. To help with the development of PL/M, the initial version of CP/M was developed. In its primitive form, CP/M was designed for handling data storage on paper tape. In those days, floppy disk storage was expensive. The most widely used method of data storage for microcomputers was paper tape. CP/M was later converted to handle floppy disks. A text editor, assembler, and debugger were also added to allow for the development of machine language programs.

One of the biggest appeals of CP/M is the wide availability of applications software written to run under that operating system. Since conversion of applications software from CP/M-80 to CP/M-86 is relatively simple, it is anticipated that a large volume of software will be available for 16 bit microprocessors running CP/M.

CP/M does present some disadvantages, however. One of these is documentation that many users find difficult to understand. Another disadvantage is that CP/M generally is not as easily mastered by first time computer users as are other operating systems. Finally, CP/M presents certain limitations when working with large capacity hard disk systems.

Digital Research is currently working to overcome these limitations, and expects to announce new versions of CP/M-80 and CP/M-86 sometime in 1982.

UCSD p-System

The UCSD p-System is the third operating system currently available for the IBM PC. The p-System was developed at the Institute for Information Science at the University of California in San Diego in the mid 1970's.

The p-System was first licensed and distributed through the office of the regents of the University of California in the late 1970's. Sole distribution rights were subsequently granted by the office of the regents to SofTech Microsystems, a subsidiary of SofTech Inc.

The p-System is quite different from PC DOS and CP/M-86. While CP/M operates on five different microprocessors (8080, 8085, 8086, 8088, and Z80) and PC DOS operates on five others (Z8000, 68000, 8080, 8086, and the 8088), the p-System will operate on over 15 different mini and microcomputer microprocessors. These include the following:

Intel 8080, 8085, 8086, 8088
Digital Equipment LSI-II, PDP-II
Mos Technology 6502
Motorola 6800, 6809, 68000
Texas Instruments 9900
Zilog Z80, Z8000
Western Digital Microprocessors

Obviously, the main advantage to the p-System is that programs written under this system will run on a much larger variety of computers than programs written under CP/M-86 or PC DOS.

The p in p-System is an abbreviation for **pseudocode.** The pseudocode or **p-code** is the code produced when the programs written in the languages supported by the USCD p-System are **compiled**. The three primary languages currently supported under the USCD p-System are PASCAL, FORTRAN, and BASIC.

When a program is written in a version of PASCAL, BASIC, or FORTRAN which is supported under USCD p-System, that program (whatever the language) is compiled or translated into universal p-code instructions instead of into machine language. The p-code is then translated into machine language by a **P-machine emulator,** which is a program that translates p-code into instructions that can be directly executed by the microprocessor.

Each microprocessor that is supported under the UCSD p-System requires a different P-machine emulator. UCSD p-code uses the same instruction set as is used with Western Digital's microprocessor chips. Therefore, p-code will execute directly with Western Digital microprocessor chips, and no P-machine emulator is required.

The UCSD p-System is then basically unchanged among the different microprocessors supported under the system. The differences lie in the fact that the P-machine emulators are customized for each separate microprocessor.

The obvious advantage to the p-System is the compatibility of programs written under this system. A compiled program written under the p-System for the Apple will run under a PDP-11, Tandy, IBM PC, or any other computer that has a P-machine emulator.

Compiled vs. Interpreted Language

Computer languages are often distinguished as being either **compiled** or **interpreted** languages.

A compiled language program consists of the **source code** and the **compiled code**. The source code consists of the program statements in their original form. For example, the following is a line of source code from a program written in the CBASIC compiled language.

```
100 INPUT "ENTER TODAY'S DATE:"; DATE.1
```

The source code is processed by a program known as a **compiler** into the compiled code. The compiled code is very similar to the machine language used by the microprocessor. The compiled code is the code actually used when a compiled program is run. A program known as a **run-time monitor** is used to run the compiled program.

An interpreted language consists of only the source code. The source code is translated line-by-line directly into machine language instructions. The Microsoft BASIC language that is standard on the IBM PC is an interpreted language.

One advantage of interpreted languages over compiled language is that interpreted language programs are more easily developed. When working with interpreted languages, a programmer need only write a program, enter it, run it, and alter it as his leisure. When working with a compiled language, the source code must be recompiled every time it is edited. This can be frustrating during the program debugging process.

One advantage of compiled languages over interpreted languages is that execution time is much faster. The compiled code is much closer to the machine language than the source code. Since interpretation is not necessary, execution of compiled code is much faster.

Monochrome Display

The video display or CRT allows communication between the operator and the computer. IBM's Monochrome Display uses a black and white picture tube with a green phosphor to produce a black and green display. A black and green video display tends to lessen eye fatigue.

The IBM Monochrome Display is about the same size as a 12 inch black and white television set.

The Monochrome Display gets its power from the System Unit. The AC power cable from the Monochrome Display will connect directly into the power supply outlet located on the rear of the System Unit. This allows the on/off switch on the System Unit to control the power to both the System Unit and the Monochrome Display.

The Monochrome Display also has a video signal cable which connects into the Monitor/Printer Adapter on the right side of the rear of the System Unit.

The IBM Monochrome Display allows for a display of 25 lines of 80 characters each. The characters output by the IBM Monochrome Display are very sharp and easily read by the operator, thereby preventing eye strain.

The IBM Monochrome Display outputs a character with matrix dimensions of 7 (horizontal) by 9 (vertical) in a 9 by 14 matrix. This additional area allows lower case letters with descenders (such as y or p) to retain their normal appearance.

The characteristics of the IBM Monochrome Display are given in Table 1-9.

IBM CPS-80 Printer

The IBM CPS-80 Printer is actually a version of the Epson MX-80 printer. This printer has an output speed of 80 characters per second in any of several styles of dot matrix print.

The IBM CPS-80 Printer will accept forms with a minimum width of 4 inches and a maximum width of 10 inches. The maximum paper thickness accepted by the IBM printer is 3 plies or .012 inches.

Paper is fed into the IBM printer from the rear of the unit. The unit's ribbon is enclosed in a removable cartridge. Each ribbon has a print capacity of 3 million characters which translates to approximately 10 hours of continuous use.

The IBM printer uses a bidirectional, 9-wire printhead. The print head has a life expectancy of 30 million inpressions. The printhead can easily be replaced by the operator.

A 9 by 9 dot matrix pattern is used to form characters. Character sizes may range from 5 to 16.5 characters per inch (CPI). On an 8 inch line width, these pitch sizes (5, 8.25, 10 and 16.5) will produce a maximum of 40, 66, 80, and 132 characters respectively.

Table 1-9. IBM Monochrome Display Features

IBM Monochrome Display	
Size:	Height: 11 in. 280 mm Width: 15 in. 380 mm Depth: 14 in. 350 mm Weight: 17 lbs. 7.9 kg.
Video Screen Characteristics;	Diagonal: 11.5 in. 292 mm P-39 Slow Green Phosphor
Cables:	AC Power Cable Video Cable (with 9 pin D-connector)
Features:	1. 80 x 25 Display 2. 7 x 9 characters with descenders in a 9 x 14 character box. 3. Direct Drive Video 4. Screen refreshment at 50 hz; 720 horizontal, 350 vertical resolution.

The IBM printer offers 3 different printing styles; normal, double, and emphasized. Normal printing involves one strike of the print head per character. Double printing involves a double strike of the print head for each character. Emphasized printing involves a single strike for the character after which the paper is stepped up by a fraction of an inch, and a single strike is again made. Emphasized printing gives the appearance of a bold character, which adds to the versatility of the printer.

Printers other that the IBM CPS-80 may be used with the PC. Parallel printers may be connected via either the Monochrome Display/Printer Adapter or the Printer Adapter cards. Serial printers can be connected via the Asynchronous Communications Adapter.

Table 1-10. IBM CPS-80 Printer Features

IBM CPS-80 Features	
Manufacturers:	Epson America Inc.
Model No:	MX-80
Introduction Date:	1979 by Epson
Size:	Height: 4.2 in. 107 mm Width: 14.7 in. 374 mm Depth: 12.0 in. 305 mm Weight: 12 lbs. 5.5 kg.
Output Speed:	80 CPS (characters per second)
Interface:	Parallel (Centronics Standard)
Forms:	Sprocket feed paper Minimum width 4 in. 102 mm Maximum width 10 in. 254 mm Maximum thickness 3 ply; .012 in.
Power:	120 v. AC, 60 Hz - 1 amp max.
Characteristics:	1. 9-pin dot matrix print head. 2. Bidirectional printing with logic seeking. 3. 9 x 9 dot characters, 96 ASC II characters, 9 int'l symbols, 64 graphic characters. 4. Black ribbon cartridge (3 million character life expectancy). 5. Paper-out sensor. 6. Self-test.

Table 1-10. IBM CPS-80 Printer Features (Cont.)

IBM CPS-80 Features	
Software Controlled Features:	1. Print Sizes: Name / Pitch / Max. chars. per line Normal / 10 / 80 Enlarged / 5 / 40 Condensed / 16.5 / 132 Condensed/Enlarged / 8.25 / 66 2. Print Styles: Normal: Single strike Double: Double strike at same position. Emphasized: Single strike, stepup paper by 1/216 inches; another strike. 3. Line Spacing: Adjustable to 6, 8, or 10 lines per inch. 4. Horizontal and vertical tabbing.

Serial and Parallel Communication

Data may be sent from the computer to the receiving device (printer or video display) in two different manners; serial and parallel. In parallel communications, the 8 bits representing a character are all sent at one time to the receiving device. In serial communications, each of the 8 bits are sent one at a time to the receiving device.

Monochrome Display/Printer Adapter Card

The Monochrome Display/Printer Adapter Card is used to link the PC to both the Monochrome Display and a parallel printer.

A separate Printer Adapter card is also available which performs only the parallel printer interface functions of the Monochrome Display/Printer Adapter Card.

The only difference between the combined Display/Printer Adapter and the Printer Adapter Card are their memory locations. The starting addresses for the Display/Printer Adapter and Printer Adapter Cards are separated by 68 locations. Other than different starting memory addresses, the cards operate identically.

The Monochrome Display portion of the combined Display/Printer Adapter Card controls communications between the PC and the video display.

Although the interface to the IBM printer conforms to Centronics electrical standards, the physical connection from the printer to the interface card is made via a DB-25 connector. Centronics, one of the largest printer manufacturers, has established a method of connecting printers to which most manufacturers conform.

To connect a parallel printer to the IBM PC, an IBM Printer Cable must be used. The IBM Printer Cable has a DB-25 connector on one end and a Centronics style connector on the other end. The DB-25 connector is for the System Unit, while the Centronics type connector is for the printer. By using the IBM Printer Cable, the IBM PC can be connected to any parallel printer with a Centronics-style connector.

The reason why the DB-25 connector is used on the PC is to prevent a problem known as **crosstalk**. Crosstalk is a fairly common problem when long cables are used for parallel communication. Crosstalk occurs when the electrical signals from the cable's parallel wires interfere with each other. To eliminate crosstalk, additional wires are placed in the cable that absorb (ground) this troublesome interference.

The Display/Printer Adapter card contains 8K of ROM (which is used to hold the codes for 256 different characters) and 4K of RAM (which holds one full screen of data -- 80 characters by 25 rows). The display RAM is refreshed 50 times per second.

Two bytes of memory are used for every character displayed in the Display/Printer Adapter (as well as the Color/Graphics Monitor Adapter). The first byte is used to store the ASC II code for the character.

The second byte is known as the **attribute code.** In the Monochrome Display, the attribute code controls the following four video features:

1. Darkness of the background
2. Darkness of the foreground
3. Intensity or brightness of the character
4. Blinking or non-blinking character

The attribute byte allows the following 6 combinations on the Monochrome Display.

1. White character on a dark background (video mode).
2. Dark character on a white background (reverse video).
3. Flashing bright character on a dark foreground.
4. White character on a white background (invisible character).
5. Dark ' character on a dark background (invisible character).
6. Flashing dark character on a white background.

As mentioned previously, both the Monochrome and Color Adapter allow for 25 lines on the display. Generally, programs are written to use at most, 24 lines of display. The 25th line is known as the **status line.**

Since programs generally do not use the status line of the display, this line offers an excellent area in which to place prompts and other information directed to the operator.

The Monochrome Display/Printer Adapter uses the Motorola 6845 CRT Controller to interface to the video display (as does the Color/Graphics Monitor Adapter). The 6845 is software controlled. This means that a program can directly control the output to the screen. For example, a program could be implemented to restrict the screen area to a size smaller than 25 x 80.

Table 1-11. IBM Monochrome Display/Printer Adapter Features

IBM Monochrome Display/Printer Adapter	
Size:	Height: 4 in. 102 mm Width: 14 in. 357 mm Depth: .25 in. 6.3 mm
Location:	System Unit Expansion Slot (generally slot 2)
Characteristics:	1. Display a. 80 x 25 or 40 x 25 text modes b. Normal, reverse, flashing, high-intensity modes c. Motorola 6845 CRT controller d. 4K RAM display buffer e. 8K ROM for 256 character codes 2. Printer a. 8 bit parallel port (Centronics compatible) b. Acknowledge, Busy, Paper Out, and Select signals c. Allows use of any Centronics compatible printer device d. 12 TTL buffered output points e. 5 input ports readable under program control f. 25 pin D-connector (female) used

Color Graphics Monitor Adapter

The main difference between the Color/Graphics Monitor Adapter and the Display/Printer Adapter is that the Color/Graphics board can provide for color, while the Display/Printer board cannot.

The Color/Graphics Monitor Adapter can be used with a color monitor or a color television set when an RF modulator is supplied.

The Color/Graphics Adapter operates under two principal methods of operation; the **alphanumeric (A/N)** or text mode and the **all points addressable (APA)** graphics mode. Each of these two primary modes includes several secondary operating modes.

A/N Mode

The A/N mode operates with a video output of 25 lines of 40 characters each when used with a television set, low-resolution monitor, or high resolution monitor. A video output of 25 lines of 80 characters each is available with high resolution monitors.

In the monochrome mode of the A/N mode, characters can be displayed in reverse, high intensity, and blinking formats. In the color mode, up to 16 foreground (or character) colors can be supported on any 1 of 8 background colors. The color mode also supports blinking characters.

The colors that may be attained through the use of the Color/Graphics Adapter are listed in Table 1-12. The numbers used in BASIC to attain the color are given in column 1. The primary colors which make up the color are given in the last 4 columns of Table 1-12.

The sixteen colors that can be obtained are all combinations of the three primary colors (red, green, and blue), and the intensity signal. Electronic color mixing is somewhat different from photographic color mixing, in that green (not yellow) is the third primary color.

The three primary colors produce eight different colors (0-7 in

Table 1-12). The intensity signal results in a different tint for each of these eight colors (8-15 in Table 1-12).

Colors 8 thru 15 in Table 1-12 may not be available with certain monitors or televisions that cannot detect the intensity control.

APA Mode

The APA (all points addressable) mode allows a program to control each dot on the video display. The APA primary mode supports three secondary modes; the **high resolution** mode, a **medium resolution** mode, and a **low resolution** mode.

Table 1-12. Color/Graphics Adapter Available Colors

Color No.	Color Name	Red	Green	Blue	Intensity Signal
0	Black	N	N	N	N
1	Blue	N	N	Y	N
2	Green	N	Y	N	N
3	Cyan	N	Y	Y	N
4	Red	Y	N	N	N
5	Magenta	Y	N	Y	N
6	Brown	Y	Y	N	N
7	Light Grey	Y	Y	Y	N
8	Dark Grey	N	N	N	Y
9	Light Blue	N	N	Y	Y
10	Light Green	N	Y	N	Y
11	Light Cyan	N	Y	Y	Y
12	Light Red	Y	N	N	Y
13	Light Magenta	Y	N	Y	Y
14	Yellow	Y	Y	Y	Y
15	White	Y	Y	Y	Y

Y = Yes N = No
Colors 8-15 may not be available on some monitors and TV's.

In the high resolution mode, the screen is divided into 640 dots horizontally by 200 dots vertically. Medium resolution consists of 320 dots horizontally by 200 dots vertically. Low resolution consists of 160 dots horizontally by 200 dots vertically.

Video Devices For The Color/Graphics Monitor Adapter

Four types of video devices can be used with the Color/Graphics Monitor Adapter; a television set, a B & W monitor, a color monitor, or an RGB color monitor.

An **RF modulator** must be used to connect a television set to the Color/Graphics Monitor Adapter. The RF modulator is a device which converts video signals into TV channels.

When using a TV set for video output, only the 40 by 25 mode can be used. The 80 x 25 screen format is not available.

Asynchronous Communications Adapter

The asynchronous communications adapter allows the IBM PC to communicate with other devices, such as other computers, printers, and modems.

Asynchronous communication refers to a method of data transmission, where information is sent to the receiving device one bit at a time with additional information included which gives the starting and stopping points of each character. In other words, asynchronous communication consists of sending data in serial form from the sending device to the receiving device at non-standard timing intervals.

The asynchronous communications adapter can be placed in any one of the five expansion slots. The adapter includes a DB-25 (25 pin) connector that extends from the rear of the System Unit.

The features of the asynchronous communications adapter are listed in Table 1-13.

Table 1-13. Asynchronous Communications Adapter

IBM Asynchronous Communications Adapter	
Size:	Height: 4 in. 102 mm Width: 5 in. 127 mm Depth .25 in.
Components:	1. INS 8250 Asynchronous Communications Element (ACE) 2. ACE Support Circuiting 3. DB-25M connector on card extending from rear of System Unit. 4. Jumper block for RS-232C or 25 ma. current loop (TTY compatible)
Characteristics:	1. Fully software controllable 2. 50-9600 baud

Chapter 2. Installing The IBM PC

Introduction

In this chapter, we will explain in detail the steps necessary for setting up the IBM PC.

IBM describes the IBM PC as a customer set-up machine. IBM has simplified the installation procedures for the IBM PC to the point where almost anyone can set the unit up on his own. Set-up involves merely unpacking the various system components and peripherals and attaching the necessary cables and connectors.

Unpacking Your IBM PC

The IBM System Unit, Keyboard Unit, and Monochrome Display are all securely packaged in sturdy cardboard cartons with packaging materials such as corner braces and foam cushions for protection.

The steps for unpacking the IBM System Unit, Keyboard Unit, Monochrome Display, and 80 CPS Matrix Printer are pictured in Illustrations 2-1, 2-2, 2-3, and 2-4 respectively.

Illustration 2-1. Unpacking The System Unit

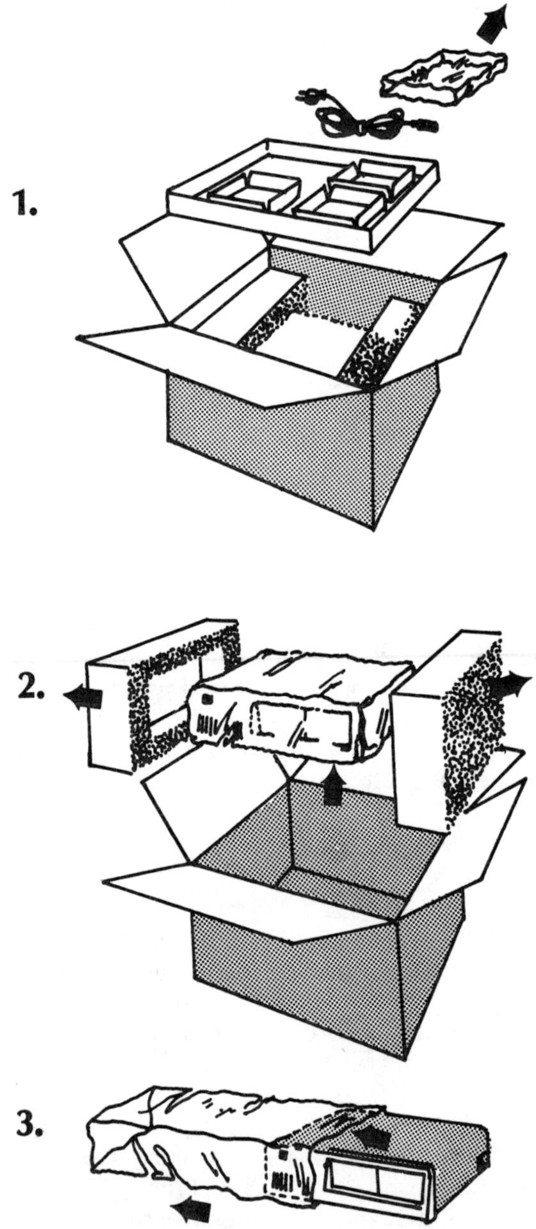

Illustration 2-2. Unpacking the Keyboard Unit

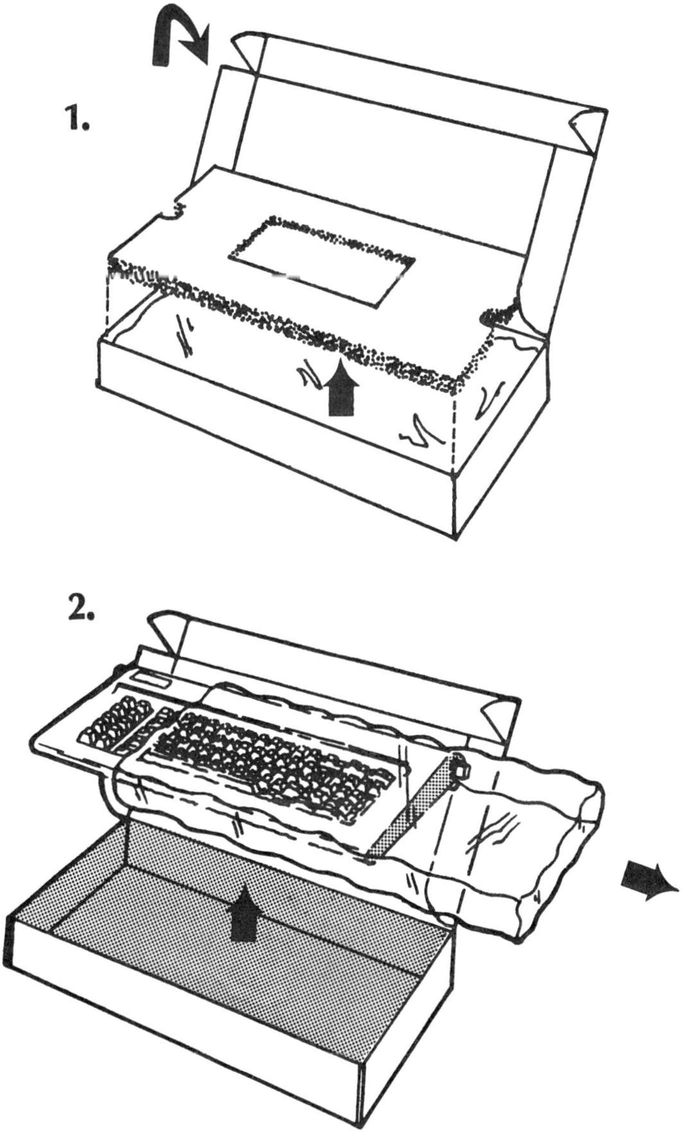

Illustration 2-3. Unpacking The IBM Monochrome Display

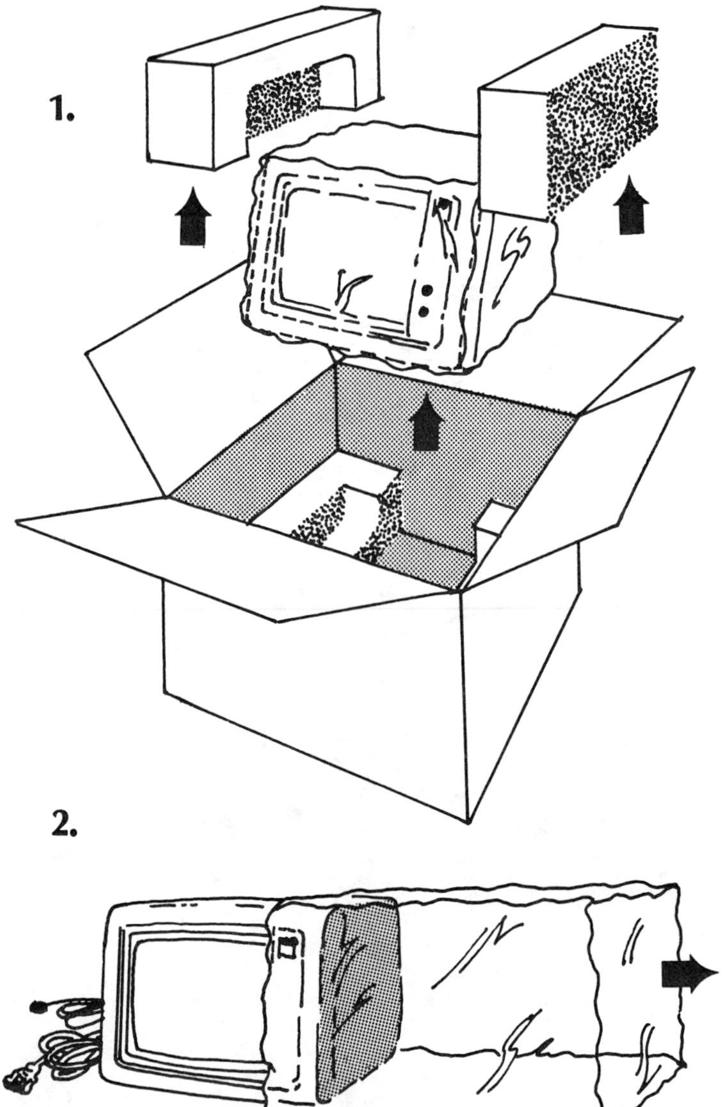

Illustration 2-4. Unpacking The IBM 80 CPS Matrix Printer

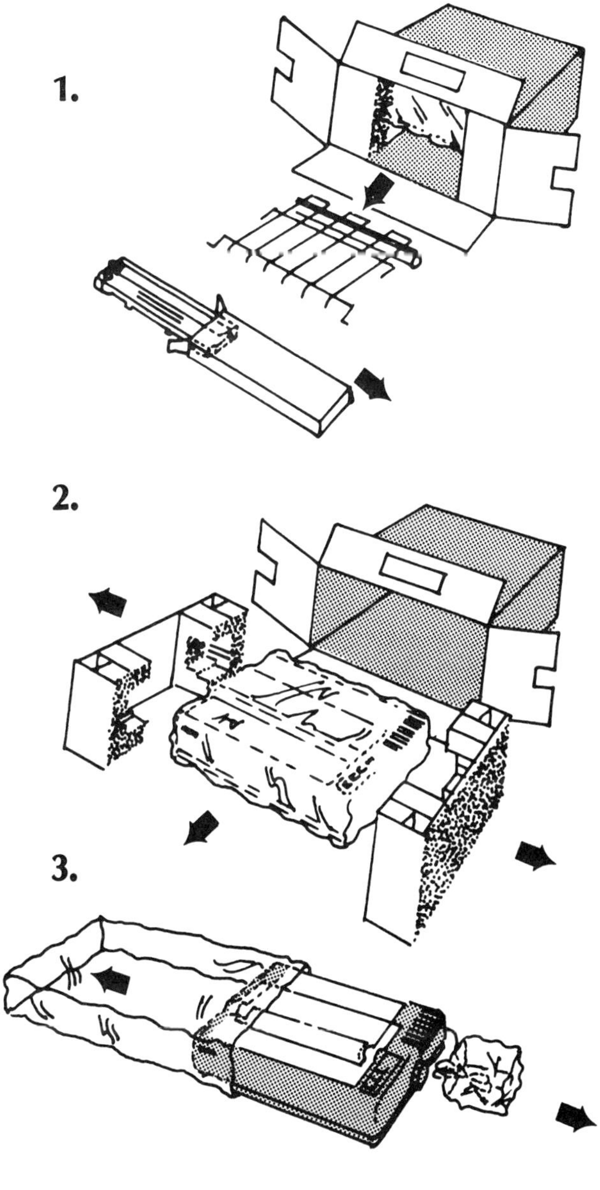

Installing The System and Keyboard Unit

Your next step after unpacking your new IBM PC will be to connect the System and Keyboard Units and then plug these in.

If you ordered your IBM PC with a built-in disk drive, a piece of tape will be fastened on the door of the disk drive. Your first step will be to remove this tape.

Then, you should lift the lever on the disk drive door which will open the drive. A piece of cardboard will be inserted in the drive. This was placed in the drive as protection during shipping. Remove this piece of cardboard as shown in Illustration 2-5.

Illustration 2-5. Removing Shipping Cardboard From Built-In Disk Drive

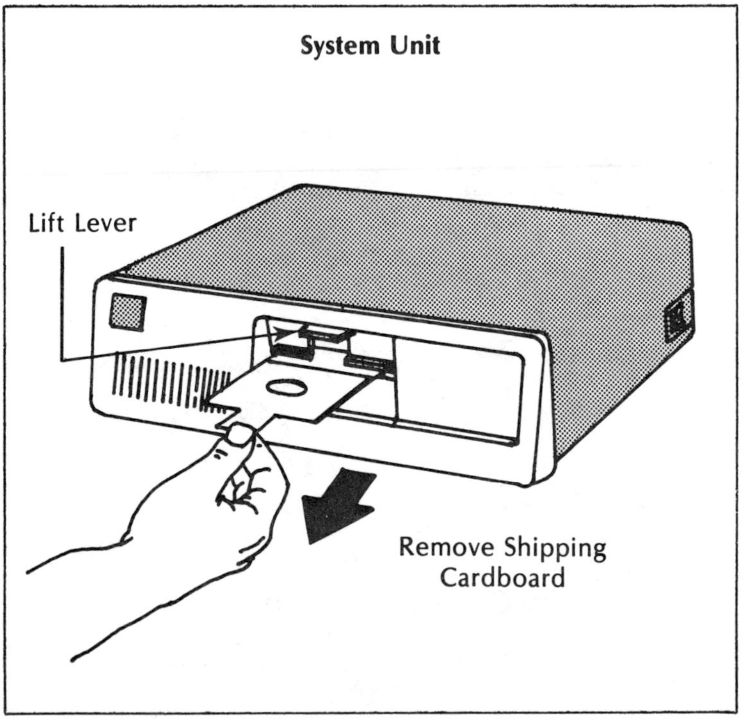

After the cardboard has been removed from the disk drive, you should place the System Unit and Keyboard Unit on your intended work area. Connect the coded cable to the rear panel of the System Unit as shown in Illustration 2-6.

Connecting The System Unit Power Cord

Before connecting the power cord, be certain that the System Unit's Power Switch is in the Off position. The On/Off switch location is shown in Illustration 2-7.

Now that you are certain that the System Unit's On/Off switch is positioned to Off, you can connect the power cord to the System Unit. After the power cord has been connected to the System Unit, you can plug it into a standard outlet. This procedure is pictured in Illustration 2-8.

Illustration 2-6. Connecting The Keyboard Unit To The System Unit

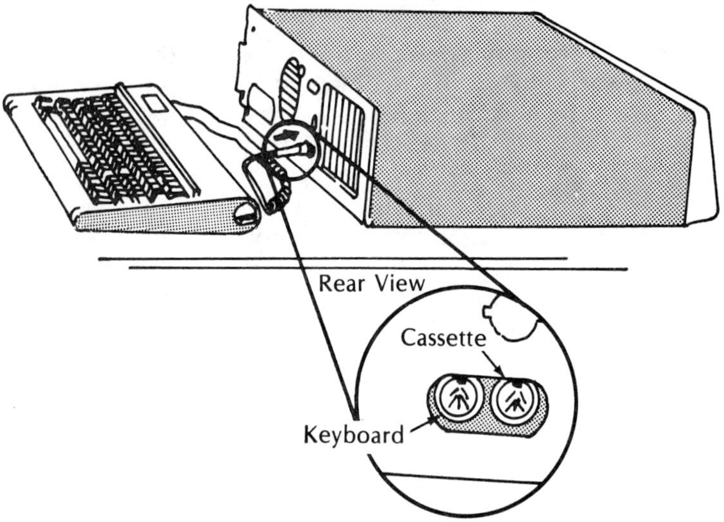

System Unit

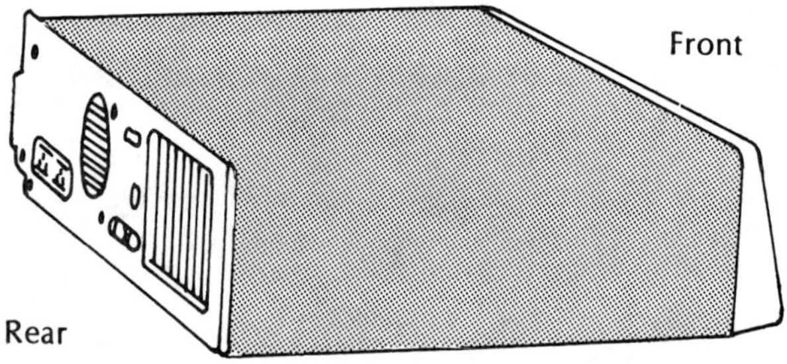

Illustration 2-7. On/Off Switch

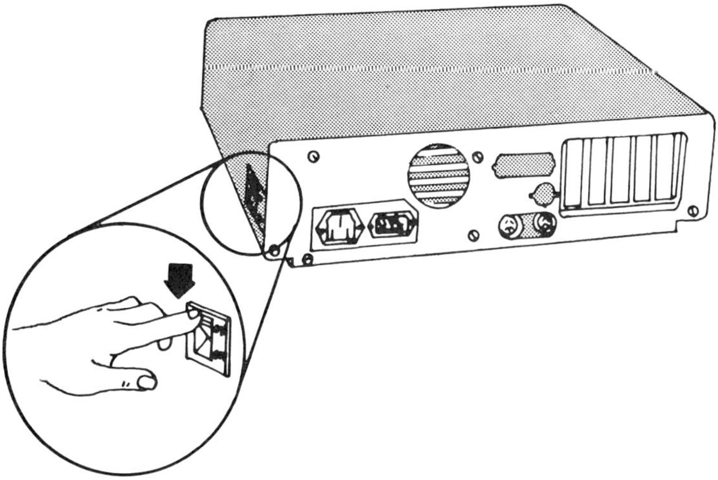

Illustration 2-8. Connecting The Power Cord

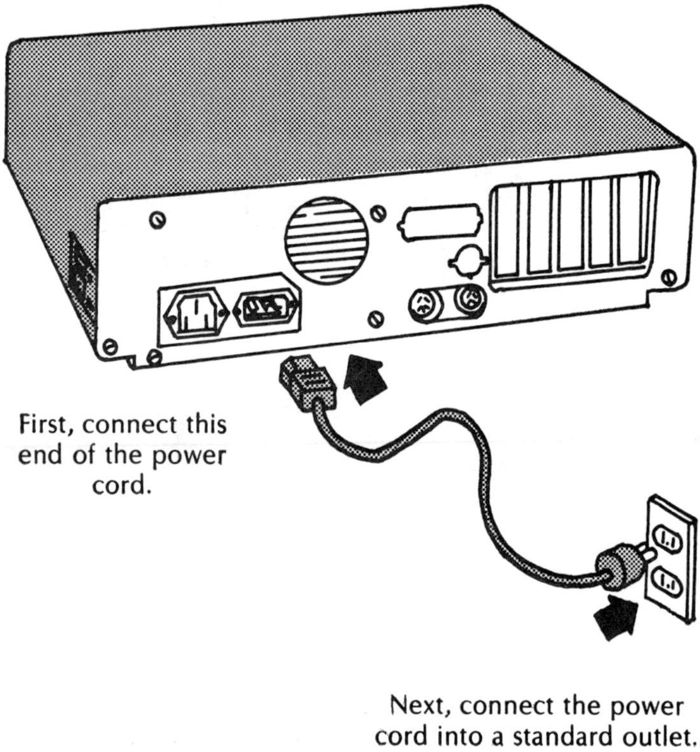

Mini Power-On Self-Test

When you turn on the power to the System Unit, the system will perform what IBM calls a Mini Power-On Self-Test.

The test is exceedingly simple from a user's point of view. If one short beep is heard by the user, the test has indicated that the system checks out. If more than one beep is heard, the user should return the IBM PC to the outlet where he purchased it.

Installing Options

Once you have completed the Mini Power-On Self-Test, you will have finished installing the basic core of your IBM PC system.

You will then be ready to install any peripherals and/or options. The installation of options and peripherals should follow the sequence listed below:

1. 16K Memory Expansion Kit
2. Disk Drives
3. Any other options

Specific installation instructions are provided by IBM for each available option.

Illustration 2-9. Rear Panel Diagram of IBM PC

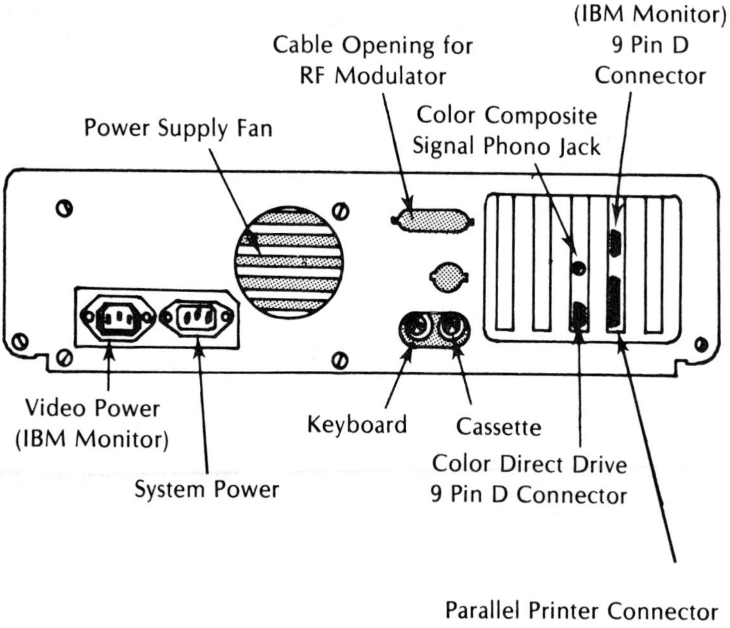

Keyboard and Monitor Adjustment

Now that you have installed the System Unit, keyboard, peripherals, and options, you are ready to test your IBM PC. However, before performing this test you may wish to adjust the keyboard and monitor.

Keyboard adjustment is pictured in Illustration 2-10. The keyboard has two different positions, the tilt position and the level position. You may wish to experiment with both positions to determine which is most comfortable.

Keyboard adjustment is a simple matter. Just turn the adjustable legs at either side to either the tilt or the level position as shown in Illustration 2-10.

Monitor adjustment is also a very simple matter. The IBM Monochrome Display has two controls located on its right hand side. These are pictured in Illustration 2-11. Use these controls to adjust the monitor's brightness and contrast to the desired levels.

Illustration 2-10. Keyboard and Monitor Adjustment

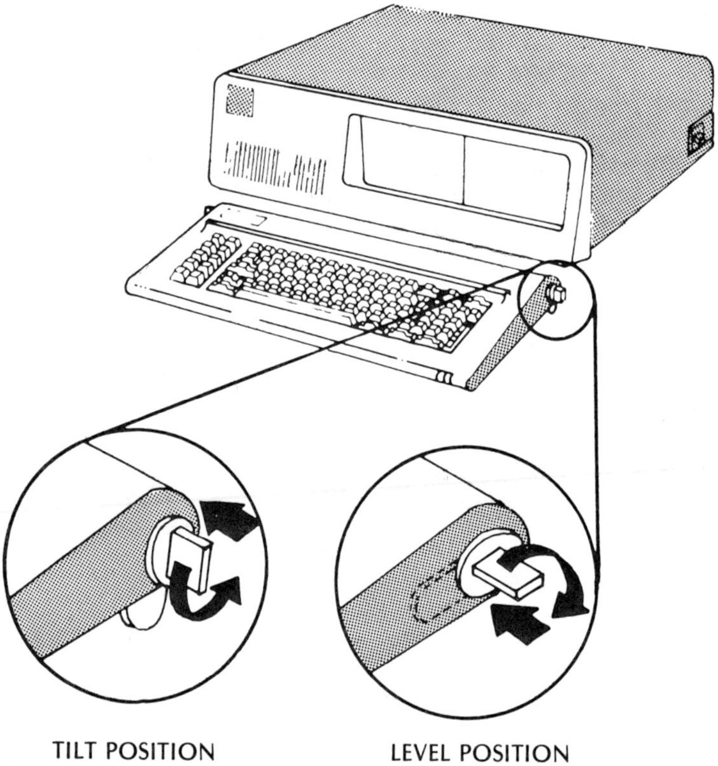

TILT POSITION
Push in firmly and turn counter clockwise.

LEVEL POSITION
Push in firmly and turn clockwise.

Illustration 2-11. IBM Monochrome Display Contrast and Brightness Controls

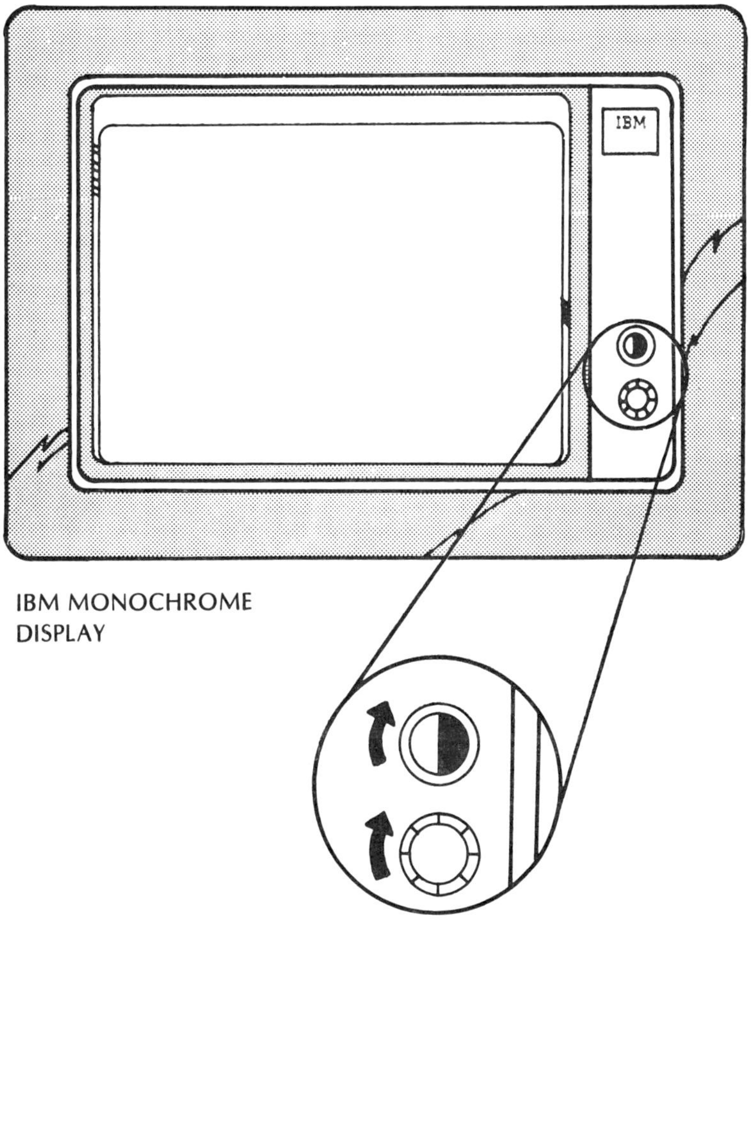

Power-On Self-Test

When your IBM PC is first turned on, a power-on self-test is performed, which involves a series of 14 tests. If any errors are found, these will be immediately reported to the user.

These tests include examinations of the 8088 microprocessor, the internal ROM, the main memory, the video display adapter card, the keyboard, the cassette recorder (if connected), and the disk drive system.

These tests may take anywhere from 5 seconds to 1 minute depending on the amount of memory in the system.

The power-on self-test is undertaken when the IBM PC is first turned on. When the System Unit's On/Off switch is first turned on, the following will occur if the test is successful.

1. The cursor will appear on the screen for about 10 seconds.

2. After the memory has been tested, a short beep will be emitted.

3. The message "IBM Personal Computer" will then appear on the video screen.

If the preceding events do not occur during the power-on test, it will be an indication that there is a problem with the system. Chapter 3 includes a description of the procedures to be undertaken to determine that problem.

When the IBM PC is restarted from the keyboard with the Ctrl-Alt-Del sequence of keys, the system tests will be dropped, and start-up will be much faster.

Chapter 3. IBM PC Troubleshooting and Maintenance

Introduction

In this chapter, we will cover the necessary procedures for determining the source of any system failures in your IBM PC, as well as what steps should be taken to correct the problem.

Problem Determination

Problem determination is a series of steps intended to help the user analyze and possibly correct system problems. By following the steps indicated in problem determination, the user should be able to decide whether or not his PC requires service, or if he can solve the problem himself.

The problem determination procedure may require that the user load either the Diagnostic Aids Diskette or the Diagnostic Aids Cassette.

The Diagnostic Aids Diskette and Cassette contain a group of tests which help the user locate a problem within any one of four components of the system, which are known as **Customer Replaceable Units** or CRU's. The CRU's consist of the System Unit, Keyboard, Display, and Printer.

Step 1. Check Power and Cable Connections

Your first step in problem determination should be to check the power cord and cable connections. Before undertaking this check, be sure that the System Unit's on/off switch is at the off position and that the power cord has been removed from the wall outlet.

The problem may be due to a faulty wall outlet. Use a lamp or another electric appliance to test the wall outlet you are using for the IBM PC.

If the wall outlet checks out Ok, next remove and reinstall each cable connection to be certain that they are properly connected. Once all the cables have been reconnected, plug the power cord back into the wall socket and perform the power-on self-test.

If the test is successful, you have solved the problem. If not, proceed to Step 2.

Step 2. Unsuccessful Power-On Self-Test

If a power-on self-test is successful, the cursor will appear on the screen for about four seconds, a short beep will occur after the memory test, and the message, "IBM Personal Computer" will appear on the video screen.

If the test is unsuccessful, a message other than "IBM Personal Computer" may appear on the video screen as pictured in Illustration 3-1.

You may hear something other than one short beep from the System Unit. You might hear one long beep followed by one short beep, or you might not hear anything.

The possible problems and their probable causes are shown in Illustrations 3-2, 3-3, 3-4, 3-5, 3-6, and 3-7.

Step 3. Obtain Service on The Failing Unit

Once you have determined which unit is causing the problem, you should have that unit serviced by IBM or your IBM dealer. The procedures involved for obtaining service as well as the types of service agreements offered by IBM for the Personal Computer are covered later in this chapter.

Step 4. Diagnostic Aids

If you are still having a problem after completing Steps 1, 2 and 3, you should use your diagnostic aids as an aid in getting your PC serviced.

Illustration 3-1. Video Monitor Display Unsuccessful Power-On Test

Possibility

Possibility

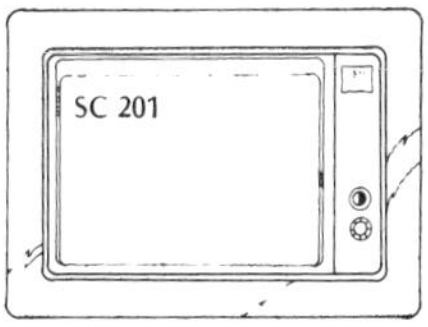

Possibility

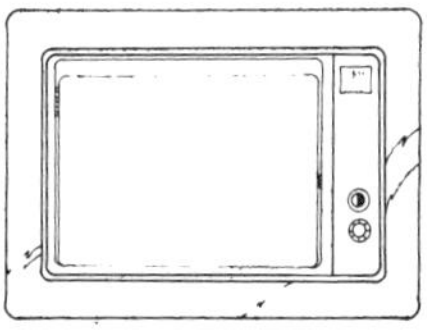

Illustration 3-2. Audio Other Than One Beep

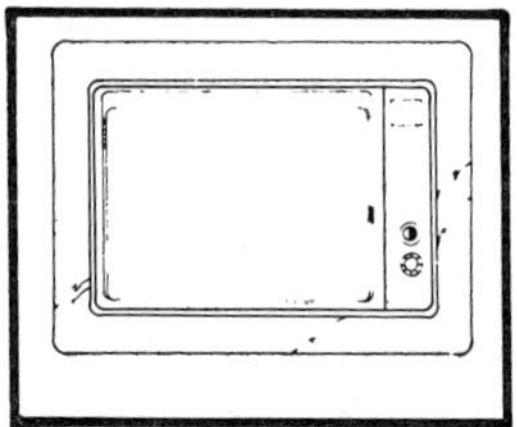

Screen Message
Does not apply. Anything may be displayed.

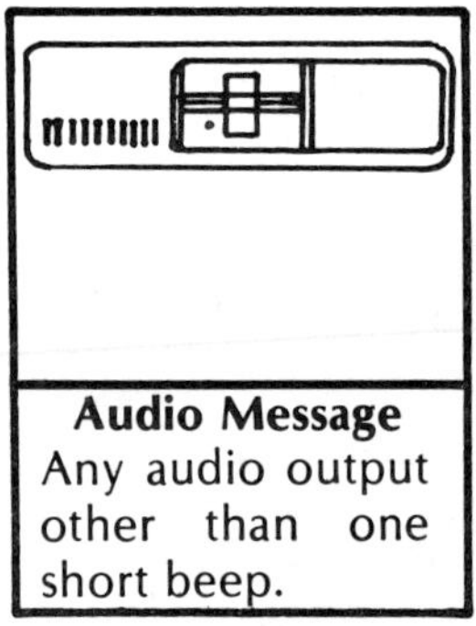

Audio Message
Any audio output other than one short beep.

Probable Cause
System Unit

Illustration 3-3. Screen Error Messages 201, 601, 131

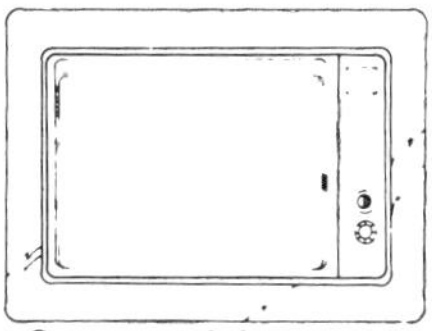

Screen Message

XXX 201
601
131
Parity Check X

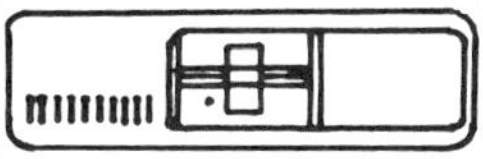

Audio Message

1 short beep

Probable Cause

System Unit

Illustration 3-4. Screen Error Message 301

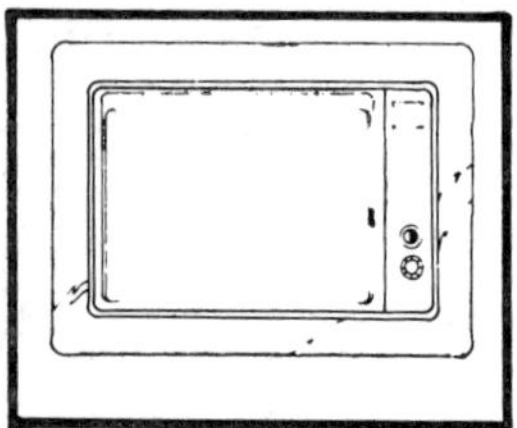

Screen Message
XXXX 301

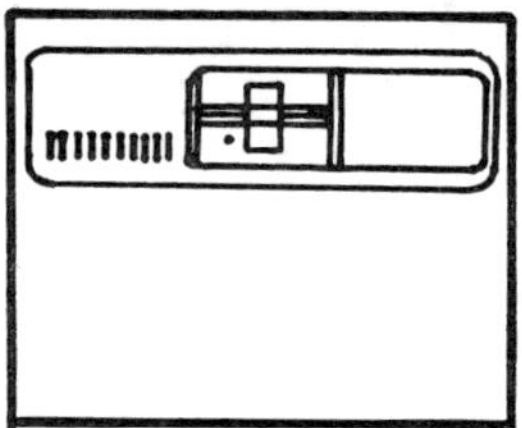

Audio Message
1 short beep

Probable Cause
Keyboard Unit*

*Perform the following checks before having the Keyboard Unit serviced.

1. Turn System Unit on/off switch to off.
2. Is Keyboard Unit connected in error to Cassette Connector?
3. Have any foreign objects fallen into the Keyboard?

If after you have had the Keyboard Unit serviced, error 301 still appears, you should have the System Unit serviced.

Illustration 3-5. Incorrect, Random Character, or No Cursor On Video Screen

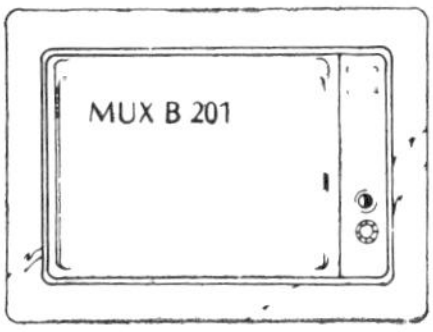

Screen Message
Wrong or random characters or no cursor.

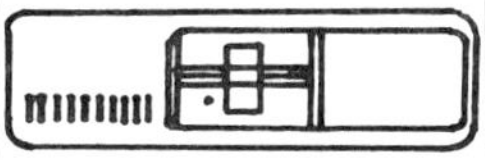

Audio Message
1 short beep.

Probable Cause
System Unit

Illustration 3-6. Screen Has Wrong Color or No Color

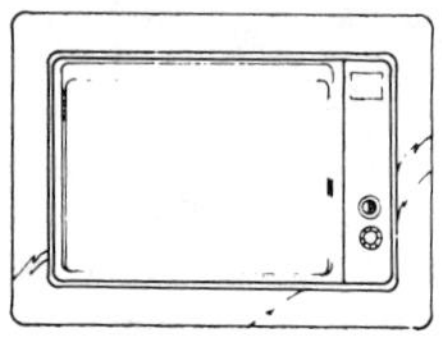

Screen Message
Screen has wrong or no color.*

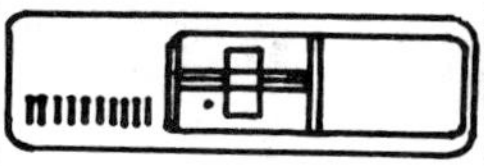

Audio Message
1 short beep

Possible Cause
System Unit.

*Color monitor only for this procedure.

Illustration 3-7. Video Screen Problems

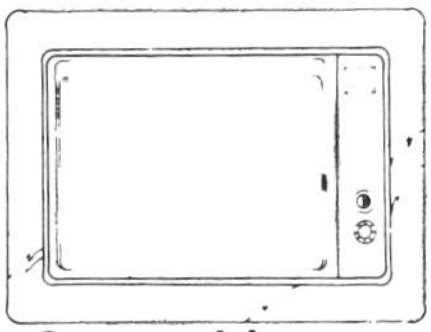

Screen Message

Video display problems such as rolling screen or shadows.

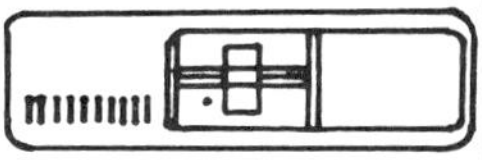

Audio Message

1 short beep.

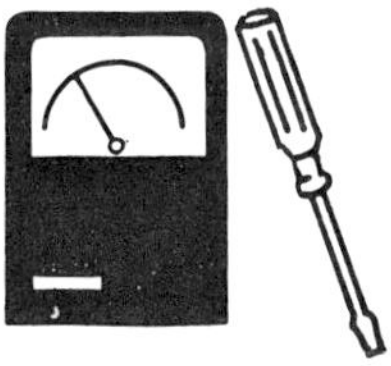

Probable Cause

Display

Note: If the problem still exists after having the video display serviced, have the System Unit serviced.

Service On Your IBM PC

Once you have determined a probable cause for your problem, you should take the following steps:

1. Notify IBM's National Support Center of the problem via its toll free number. You should be prepared to provide the serial number of the malfunctioning unit, its location, and the results of the Diagnostic Aid Program.

2. Prepare the unit for shipment in its original container. If the original container is no longer available, IBM will provide a container. However, that container must be purchased by the PC owner.

3. Remove all non-IBM devices from the unit prior to delivery to IBM.

4. Accept, unpack, and check out the replacement or the repaired units.

IBM offers service on the PC under the warranty, under a warranty extension option, under an annual option, and on a mail-in basis on a time and materials charge. These various types of service will be explained in the following sections.

Warranty Service

The warranty period for the IBM PC and its related peripherals and options is three months. Service under the warranty may be obtained by delivering the unit needing repair to an IBM Product/Service Center, or IBM Service Division designated Service location, or to an IBM authorized PC dealer. Warranty service may also be obtained by mailing the unit to the IBM National Support Center in Greencastle, Indiana. Proof of purchase from IBM or an IBM authorized dealer is required to obtain warranty service.

The following IBM service locations are planned for 1981:

Baltimore, MD	Dallas, TX
San Francisco, CA	Boston, MA
Philadelphia, PA	New York, NY
Los Angeles, CA	Chicago, IL
Seattle, WA	Detroit, MI
Houston, TX	Washington DC

Video Screen Out of Line

You may find that the output to the video monitor or television set that you are using with your IBM PC is off-line. An example of an off-line video is shown in Illustrations 3-8 and 3-9.

Either the OUT statement (with a cassette system) or the MODE command (with a diskette system) can be used to correct a situation where the video screen is out of line.

The OUT statement is used in IBM BASIC to send a byte of data to a machine output port. OUT takes the following format;

OUT n, m

where n can be any number from 0 to 65535 and m can be any number from 0 to 255.

If your video display does not have a horizontal adjustment control, and the first two or three characters do not show up on the video screen, you can issue the following statements which will shift a 40 column width display two characters to the right.

OUT 980,2: OUT 981,43

If you are using an 80 column width display, the following statements will shift the display five characters to the right.

OUT 980,2: OUT 981,85

As stated earlier, the MODE statement is used to adjust the screen display when the PC is used with a disk system. The mode command is discussed in detail in Chapter 6.

A misaligned video display can also be corrected by using the diagnostic aids diskette or cassette. When the diagnostic aids diskette or cassette is in place, press function key F8 to move the screen to the right or function key F7 to move the screen to the left.

Illustration 3-8. Screen Out of Line When Using Cassette System

OUT 980,2: OUT 981,43

OUT 980,2: OUT 981,85

Illustration 3-9. Screen Out of Line When Using Disk System

Loading The Diagnostic Aids Diskette

First of all, before loading the diagnostic aids diskette, turn the System Unit's power switch off. Next, press up on the lever on the door to drive A. The door will open. Insert the diagnostic aids diskette into drive A. Close the disk drive door by pressing down on the lever. Finally, turn the System Unit's power switch to the on position.

Loading The Diagnostic Aids Cassette

First of all, turn the power switch on the System Unit to off. Next, insert the diagnostic aids cassette and rewind it to its beginning. Turn the System Unit's power switch on.

Next, turn the volume on the cassette recorder to high, and press the recorder's play key.

Now, type the following on the keyboard:

load ld cass

and press the Enter key. The Enter key appears as follows on the PC.

Make sure that your cassette is operating. When the following message is displayed;

Id cass.B found
OK

You should enter the following command via the keyboard;

RUN

and press the Enter key.

After a minute or two, information similiar to that in Illustration 3-10 will be displayed on the video screen. If you could not load your cassette, any of the following could be the source of the problem;

Cassette Recorder Failure
Damaged Cassette
Keyboard Failure

If the diagnostic aids cassette cannot be loaded, contact IBM service or the outlet where you purchased your PC.

After the video screen containing the list of installed devices is loaded, the user can proceed with the diagnostic procedures as outlined in the section entitled, "Diagnostic Diskette:Run Diagnostic Routines".

Illustration 3-10. Video Display Upon Loading Diagnostic Aids Cassette

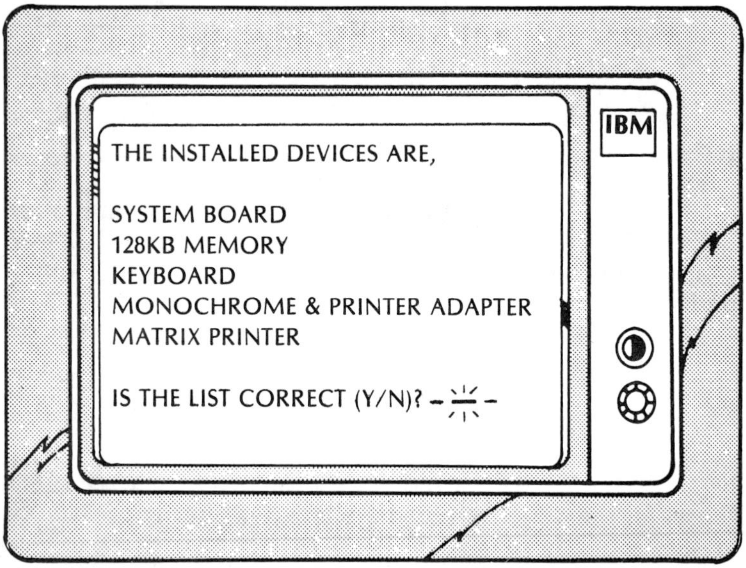

Diagnostic Diskette: Select Options

When the Diagnostic Diskette has been loaded, a video display similar to that shown in Illustration 3-11 will appear on the screen.

If this display does not appear, remove the diskette. Make certain that it actually was the diagnostic aids diskette, and that it was properly inserted. If these are not the cause of the problem, you should have your System Unit serviced.

The operator can choose any of the four options listed in Illustration 3-11.

0 - RUN DIAGNOSTIC ROUTINES
1 - FORMAT DISKETTE
2 - COPY DISKETTE
9 - EXIT TO SYSTEM DISKETTE

Illustration 3-11. Select Options

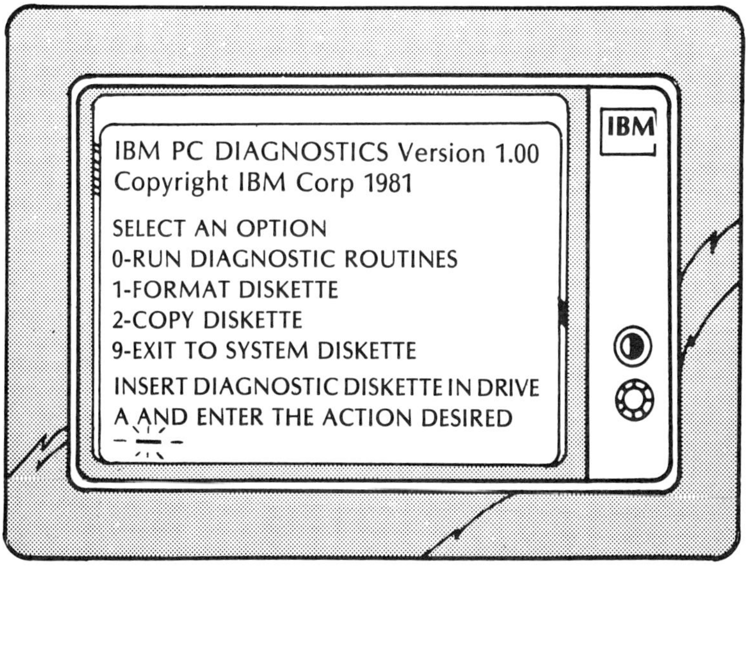

1. Format Diskette Option

If a 1 is entered as the desired option, the display shown in Illustration 3-12 will appear on your screen.

At this point, you should insert a blank diskette into drive A or B. For our purposes, we will assume that you will remove the diagnostic diskette from drive A and insert a blank diskette in its place.

Press A and then the Enter key in response to the following prompt (see Illustration 3-12).

WHICH DRIVE CONTAINS DISKETTE TO BE FORMATTED?

Illustration 3-12. Format Video Display

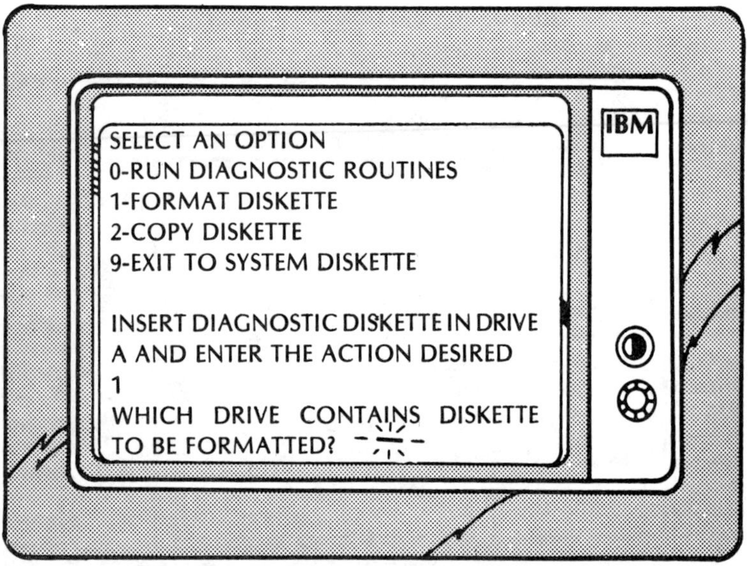

The blank diskette in drive A will then be formatted. The disk drive's in-use light will remain on while the blank diskette is being formatted. When the in-use light goes off, the blank diskette will have been formatted.

After the blank diskette has been formatted and removed, the diagnostic diskette should be inserted into drive A. Your screen should contain the message found in Illustration 3-11, SELECT OPTIONS. Here, the user can select the desired option.

0 - Run Diagnostic Routines

If the operator chooses option 0 in the video display shown in Illustration 3-11, then the diagnostic routine will be run.

Step 1. Diagnostic Routines

When the diagnostic routine is first run, a list of the components and options included in your IBM PC System will be displayed on the screen. These can include the following:

System Board
XXX KB Memory
Keyboard
Monochrome and Printer Adapter
Color/Graphics Adapter
"X" Diskette Drive(s)
Parallel Printer Adapter
Async Communications Adapter
Game Control Adapter
Matrix Printer

If the list of system components and options displayed in the screen match those contained in your system, then press the Y key followed by the Enter key. Proceed to Step 2.

If this list does not match your system's components, be certain that all of the components have been properly connected and have their power on. If this is the case (except when the printer is the component missing from the screen), press the N key followed by the Enter key. Record the error message and have the System Unit serviced.

If the printer was the missing component, check the problem determination chart for the printer (see page 99).

If the list of system components displayed on the screen did not match the actual components included in your system because the power to one of the components was off, then perform the following steps:

- Remove Diagnostic Diskette
- Turn Power Off
- Turn Power On
- Insert Diagnostic Aids Diskette
- Repeat Diagnostic Procedures

Step 2. Diagnostic Routines

After Y has been entered to complete Step 1, the video display shown in Illustration 3-13 will appear.

The operator should choose option 0 -- Run Tests One Time -- and proceed to Step 3.

Step 3. Keyboard Test

The video display shown in Illustration 3-14 should appear on your screen. If this display does not appear, press n and then Enter, record the message and have the System Unit serviced.

When this display does appear, you should press each key on your keyboard once and proceed to Step 4.

Step 4. Typematic® Test

The video display shown in Illustration 3-15 should appear on your screen. If any of the blocks in Illustration 3-14 did not

Illustration 3-13. System Checkout Display

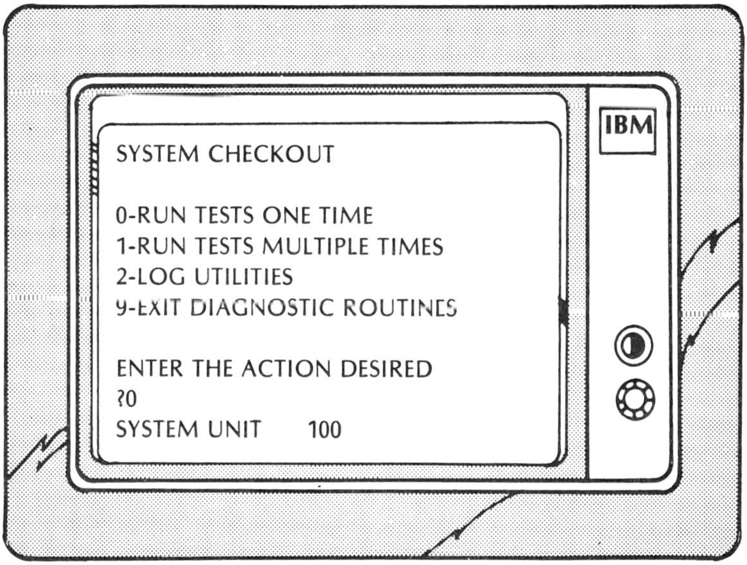

Illustration 3-14. Keyboard Test

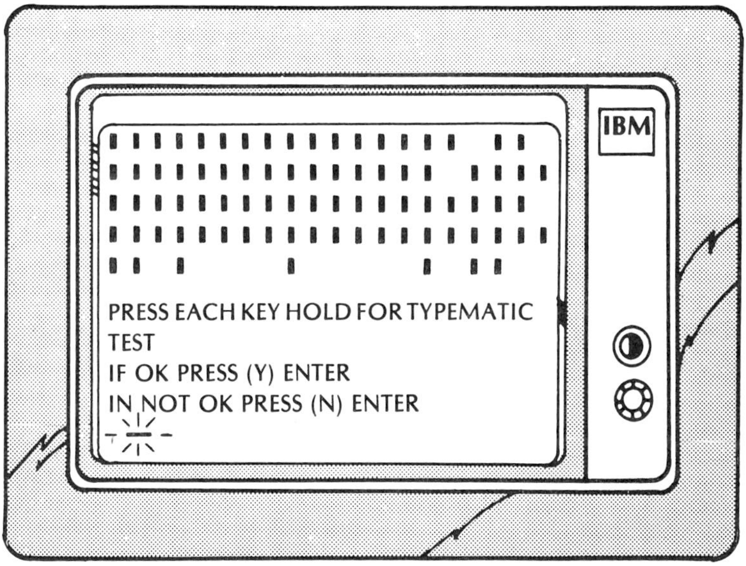

change to one of the characters in Illustration 3-15, you should have your keyboard serviced.

If your video display does match that of Illustration 3-15, you should perform IBM's Typematic® Test by pressing and holding any key on the keyboard. The corresponding key character on the video screen should flash.

If the Typematic test is successful, press Y and Enter and proceed to Step 5. If the Typematic test is unsuccessful, press N and then Enter. Record the error message, and have the System Unit serviced.

Step 5. Video Display Attributes Test

Steps 5 through 7 will apply to both black and white and color screens. We will note differences that apply to the tests for the two different screens.

The video display shown in Illustration 3-16 will appear on your screen when the diagnostic tests proceed to Step 5. If your screen matches that shown in Illustration 3-16, press Y and then Enter and proceed to Step 6. If your screen does not match the screen pictured in Illustration 3-16, press N and then Enter. Record the error message and have the System Unit serviced.

Step 6. Character Set Test 1

The video display shown in Illustration 3-17 will be displayed when the diagnostic test reaches Step 6. If your screen display matches that shown in Illustration 3-17, press Y and then Enter and proceed to Step 7. If your screen display does not match, press N and then Enter. Record the error message and have the System Unit serviced.

Illustration 3-15. Typematic® Test

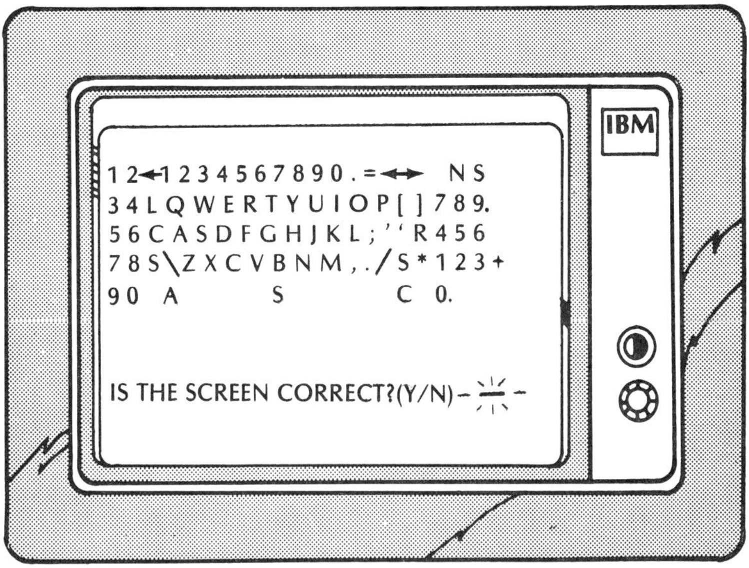

Illustration 3-16. Display Attributes Test

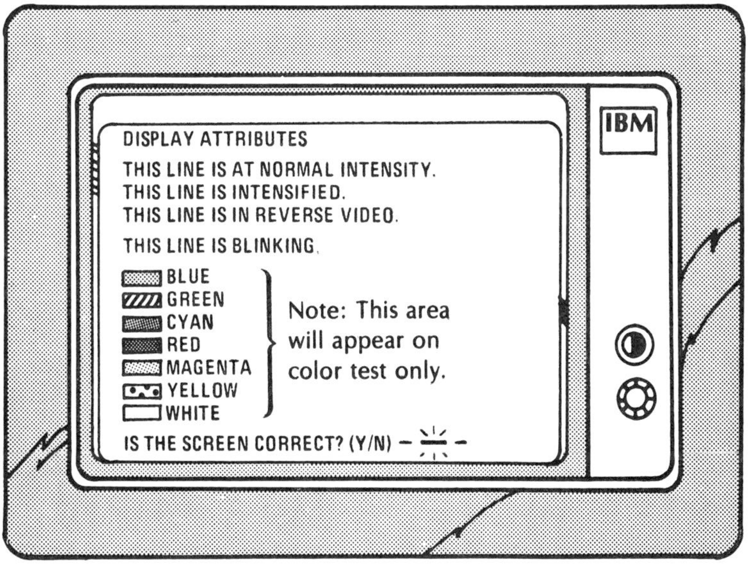

Illustration 3-17. Character Set Test 1

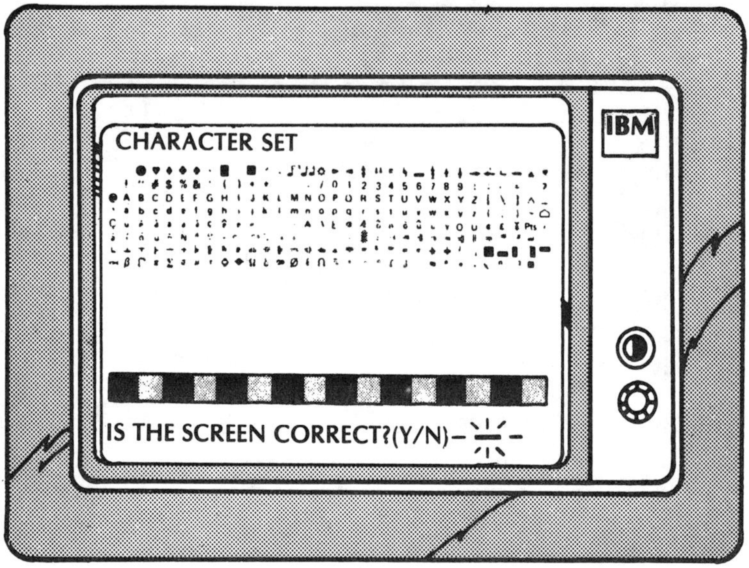

Illustration 3-18. Row/Column Display Test

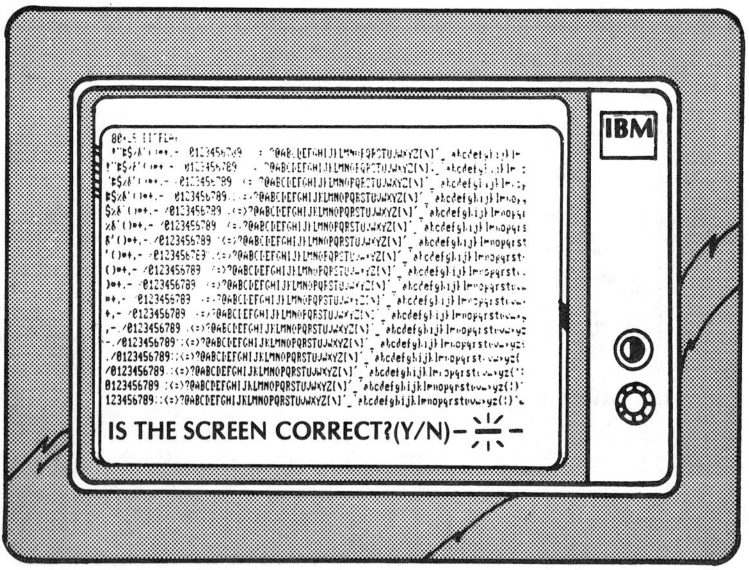

Step 7. Row/Column Display Test

When Step 7 is executed in the diagnostic test, the video display shown in Illustration 3-18 should appear on your screen. If your screen display matches that shown in Illustration 3-18, press Y and then Enter and proceed to Step 8. Otherwise, press N and then Enter. Record the error message and have the System Unit serviced. If the error message is 432, follow the procedures in Printer Problem Determination (see page 99).

Step 8. Color Monitor Row/Column Display Test

If you are using a color monitor, proceed with Steps 8 thru 13. If you are using a black and white monitor, proceed to Step 14.

Your color monitor screen display should correspond to that shown in Illustration 3-19. If it does, press Y and then Enter and proceed to Step 9. Otherwise, press N and then Enter. Record the error message and have the System Unit serviced.

Step 9. Color Set 0 Test (320 x 200 graphics)

Your display screen should match that shown in Illustration 3-20. If it does, then press Y and Enter and proceed to Step 10. If not, press N and Enter. Record the error message and have the System Unit serviced.

Step 10. Color Set 1 Test (320 x 200 graphics)

Your display screen should match that pictured in Illustration 3-21. If it does, then press Y and Enter, and proceed to Step 11. If not, press N and Enter. Record the error message and have the System Unit serviced.

Illustration 3-19. Color Monitor Row/Column Display Test

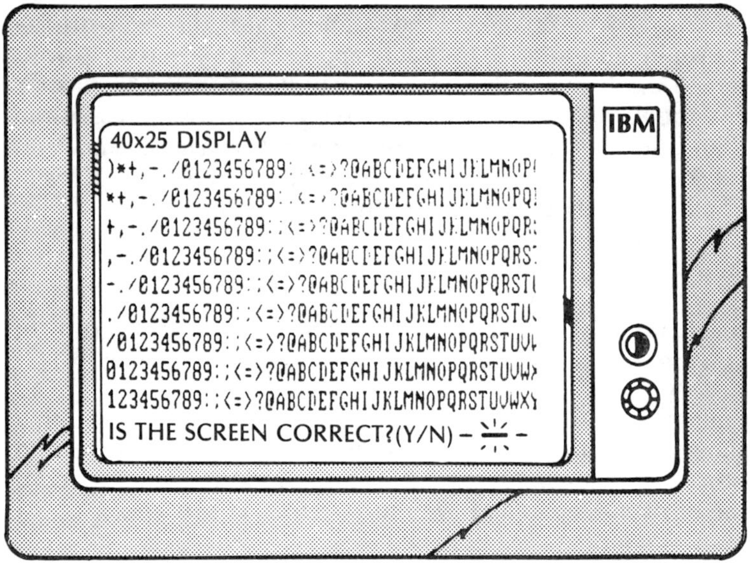

Illustration 3-20. Color Set 0 Test (320 x 200)

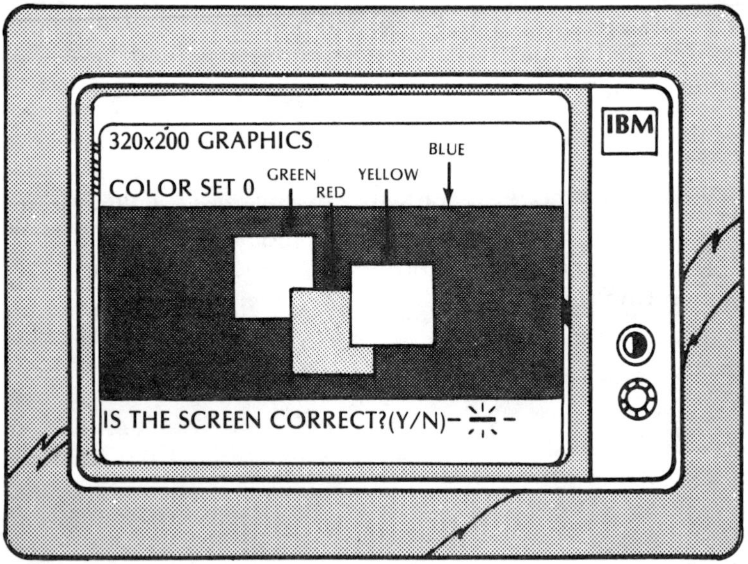

Illustration 3-21. Color Set 1 Test (320 x 200)

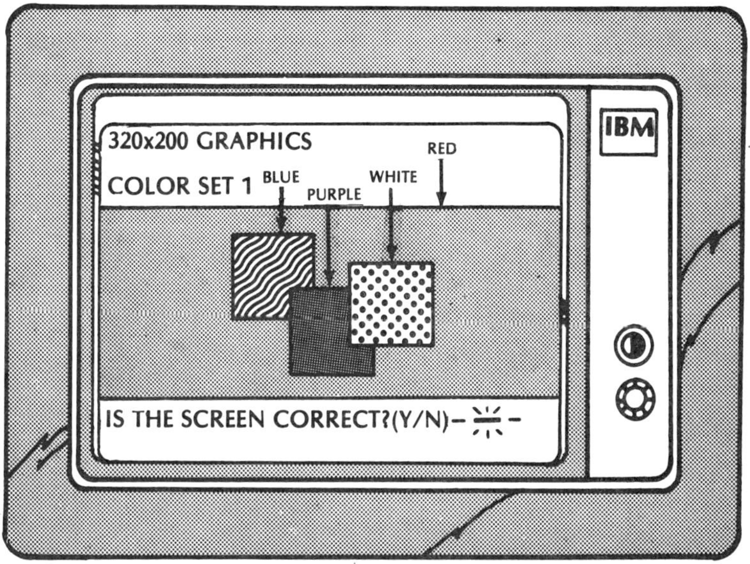

Illustration 3-22. 640/200 Graphics Test

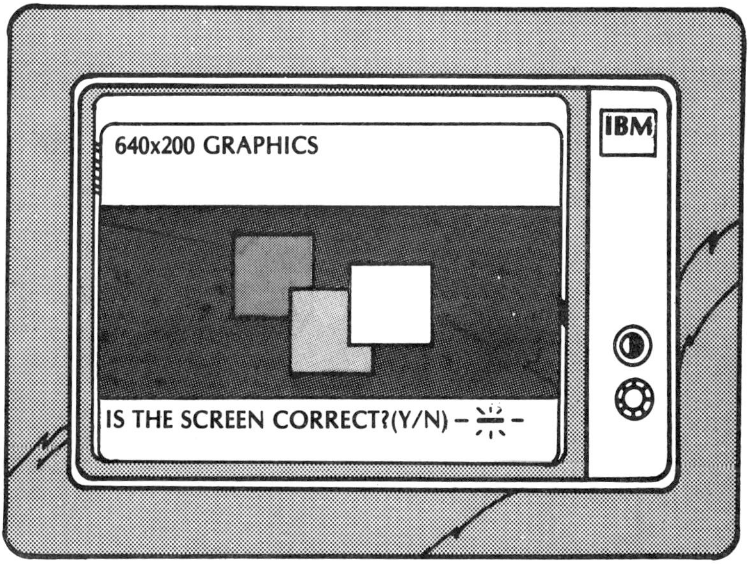

Step 11. 640 x 200 Graphics Test

Your display screen should match that shown in Illustration 3-22. If it does, then press Y and Enter, and proceed to Step 12. If not, press N and Enter. Record the error message and have the System Unit serviced.

Step 12. Video Page 0 Test

Your display screen should match that shown in Illustration 3-23. If it does, press any key and proceed to Step 13. Otherwise, press N and then Enter. Record the error message and have the System Unit serviced.

Step 13. Video Page 1 Test

Your display screen should match that shown in Illustration 3-24. Press any key to display the next video page. Continue until video page 7 appears on your screen.

If video pages 0 to 7 were displayed, press Y and then Enter, and proceed to Step 14. Otherwise, press N and then Enter. Record the error message and have the System Unit serviced.

Step 14. Remove Diagnostic Aids Diskette

Your display should match that shown in Illustration 3-25. Remove the Diagnostic Aids Diskette from drive A and insert a blank formatted diskette (scratch diskette) in its place. Proceed to Step 15.

One thing to keep in mind is that if your IBM PC contains two installed disk drives, the test will be repeated in drive B.

Step 15. Remove Scratch Diskette

When the in-use light on the disk drive goes out, continue with Step 15. A display similiar to Illustration 3-25 will appear on your screen. The operator should remove the scratch diskette.

If the error message displayed is 432, 901, or 1401, proceed with the Printer Determination Procedures. If any other error message appears, have the System Unit serviced.

Illustration 3-23. Video Page 0 Test

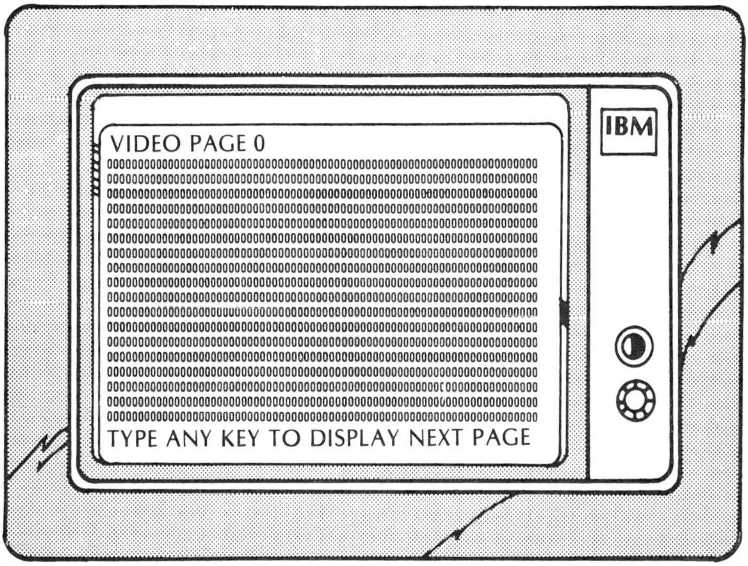

Illustration 3-24. Video Page 1 Test

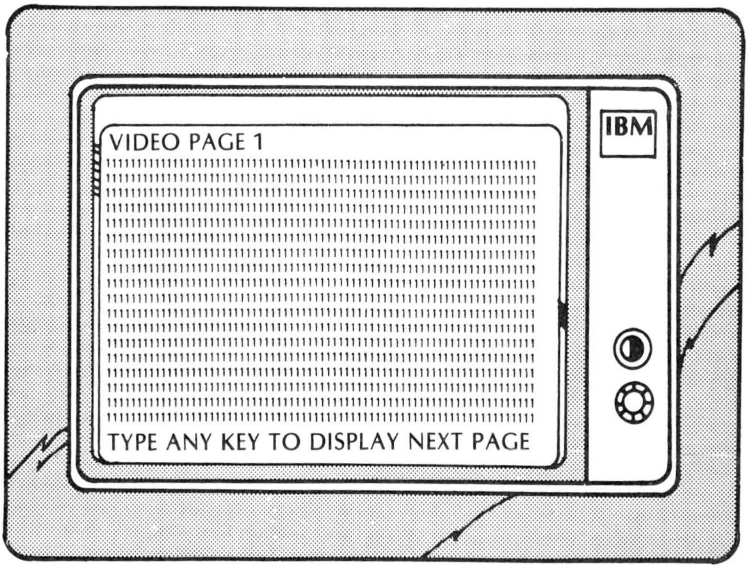

Illustration 3-25. Remove Diagnostic Aids Diskette

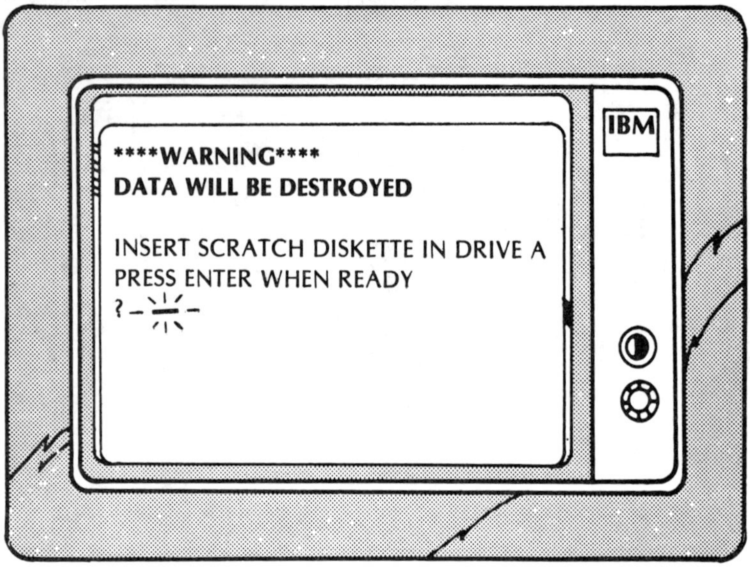

Step 16. Printer Test

If a printer is connected to your IBM PC, the following print sample should be output.

If the sample output matches, the problem determination procedure has ended, and your IBM PC should be ready to load its operating system. Otherwise, the printer and cable should be serviced.

Printer Problem Determination Procedures

Refer to Table 3-1 for possible problems that might be encountered with your printer as well as possible solutions.

The following should also be kept in mind when analyzing printer problems.

- Check the wall outlet with a lamp.
- Check to be sure the printer is plugged in.
- Check the cable connection between the printer and System Unit.
- If any control panel lights on the printer do not work, have the printer serviced.

Table 3-1. Printer Problem Determination Chart

Problem 1. Characters only partially printed or not printed at all.

Possible Cause	Corrective Action
Ribbon Worn	Install New Ribbon
Ribbon Not Properly Installed	Check Ribbon Installation
Unknown	Run self-test. If output is incorrect, have printer and cable serviced. If output is correct, reconnect cable, go to error messages.

Problem 2. Improper Forms Feed

Possible Cause	Corrective Action
Forms Not Feeding Properly	1. Forms feed path is not straight. 2. Obstruction in forms feed path. 3. Tracks adjusted improperly.
Unknown	Have printer and cable serviced.

Problem 3. Error Messages

Possible Cause	Corrective Action
Printer Not Properly Cabled	Check cable to be sure it is properly connected.
Error Message 191, 432, 901, or 1401.	Disconnect printer cable and rerun diagnostic aids. If error message repeats, have System Unit and cable serviced. Otherwise, have cable and printer serviced.

IBM Warranty Service

The warranty period on the IBM PC is 3 months. Warranty service can be obtained for the PC by delivering the unit requiring service (i.e. System Unit, keyboard, printer, etc.) to an IBM Product/Service Center, an IBM Service Division designated service location, or to an authorized IBM dealer. Warranty service can also be obtained by shipping the unit requiring service to the IBM National Support Center in Greencastle, Indiana. Proof of purchase from IBM or an IBM authorized dealer is required to obtain warranty service.

To obtain warranty service from IBM, the customer must first call the toll-free number at the National Support Center. The customer must provide the following information:

- Serial Number
- Machine Location
- Results of Diagnostic Aid Test
- Whether customer wishes to deliver unit to a service location or ship it to the National Support Center.

The warranty service offered by IBM includes the repair of the System Unit. Replacement is offered on the Monochrome Display, Matrix Printer, or Keyboard Unit. The replacement unit will be in good working order. The malfunctioning unit will become IBM's property.

The customer has the option of requesting repair of a unit IBM would otherwise replace. If this option is chosen, the repair must take place at the National Support Center, and an additional charge will be levied for the repair.

If warranty service is to be obtained at a service location, the IBM PC owner is responsible for pick-up and delivery. If the malfunctioning unit is to be mailed to the National Support Center, the IBM PC owner is responsible for shipping and insurance charges to the National Support Center, while IBM will pay the return charges.

IBM Maintenance Options

IBM offers maintenance on the PC under two separate plans:

- Warranty Extension Option
- Annual Option

The Warranty Extension Option is only available if it is selected before the warranty period expires. The Warranty Extension Option begins on the same date that the warranty takes effect and continues for 12 months. At the end of this 12 month period, the service agreement will be automatically renewed under the Annual Option. If the customer does not wish to renew the service agreement, he must withdraw the machine from the agreement.

The Annual Option may be selected during the warranty period. If the Annual Option agreement is approved by IBM, the Annual Option service agreement will begin on the day after the end of the warranty.

If the Annual Option is chosen after the warranty period has expired, the PC must be inspected at the National Support Center before the agreement can be executed. The inspection will be charged for. If repairs are needed for the unit to qualify for service, IBM will provide an estimate of their cost. If the customer authorizes these repairs, they will be performed and billed.

Warranty and Service Agreement Customer Responsibilities

During the warranty period and under the service agreements, the customer has the following responsibilities.

- Identify the malufunctioning unit by using the Diagnostic Tests.

- Notify IBM through the National Support Center of the malfunction, including the unit's serial number, location, and results of Diagnostic Tests.

- Prepare unit for shipment in the original container or its equivalent. IBM will provide shipping containers for purchase by customer.

- Remove all non-IBM devices or features prior to delivery to IBM.

- Accept, unpack, and check replacement on repaired units.

Service agreements are not transferrable upon sale of the unit.

IBM Service Locations

The following IBM service locations are planned for 1981.

Baltimore, MD
San Francisco, CA
Philadelphia, PA
Los Angeles, CA
Seattle, WA
Houston, TX
Dallas, TX
Boston, MA
New York, NY
Chicago, IL
Detroit, MI
Washington DC

Time and Materials Service

Time and materials service is only available on a mail-in basis through the National Support Center in Greencastle, Indiana.

The customer will be billed for all labor, service, parts, and transportation costs. Before service can be obtained, the customer must perform the following:

- Determine problem with Diagnostic Tests.
- Call the National Support Center
- Remove all non-IBM devices.
- Insure unit on transit.
- Check out repaired unit.

Chapter 4. Operating The IBM Personal Computer

Introduction

In this chapter, we will discuss the steps involved that will allow you to begin using your IBM Personal Computer. The power-on self-test, keyboard usage, and printer operation will be discussed in detail.

Power-On Self-Test

When you first turn on the System Unit, the power-on self-test will be performed. The time required by this test will be from 3 to 45 seconds depending upon the amount of memory contained within your system.

If the Power-On Self-Test is successful, the following events will occur.

- Cursor will appear on screen after approximately 4 seconds.
- One short beep will occur after the memory has been tested.
- The message "IBM Personal Computer" will appear on the screen.

Other information might also appear on your screen which does not apply to our discussion here.

If any of the preceding events did not occur as described above, perform the following checks:

- Turn System Unit's power off. Unplug power cord. Check all cable and cord connections.
- Check wall outlet for power with a lamp.

- Rerun Power-On Self-Test.

If the Power-On Self-Test responses are still incorrect, refer to the problem determination procedures in Chapter 3.

After the Power-On Self-Test has been successfully completed and the video screen's contrast and brightness controls are properly adjusted, your screen should resemble that shown in Illustration 4-1. If it does not, refer to the section on problem determination procedures in Chapter 3.

Illustration 4-1. Initial Screen Display

Keyboard Usage

The IBM keyboard layout is depicted in Illustration 4-2. Note that the keys outlined in gray are the same as those used on a typewriter.

In Illustration 4-3, the keys outlined in gray are keys used in writing or running programs. These are explained in Table 4-1.

In Illustration 4-4, the program function keys are outlined in gray. These are used to instruct your PC to perform certain commands. These are listed in Table 4-2.

In Illustration 4-5, the numeric keypad keys are outlined in gray. The NUM LOCK key means number lock. When this key is depressed, the numeric keypad is activated. The various numeric keypad keys are discussed in Table 4-3.

Illustration 4-2. IBM Keyboard (Typewriter Keys)

Illustration 4-3. IBM Keyboard (Program Control Keys)

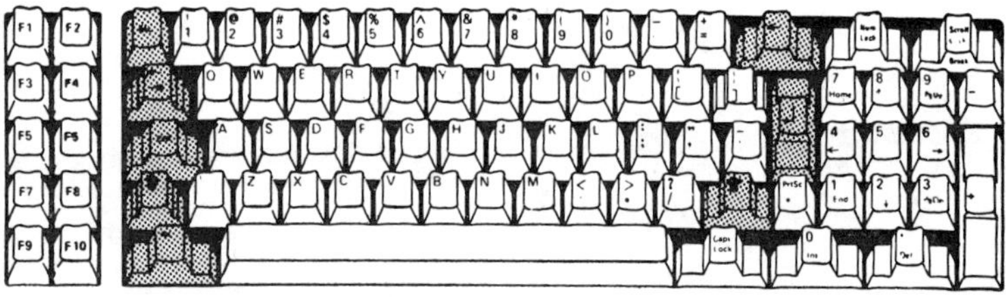

Table 4-1. Program Control Keys

Key	Explanation
ESC	Escape Key -- removes the last line that the cursor is in. However, the line is not deleted from memory.
⇤ ⇥	Tab Key -- performs a tab function much as on a typewriter. Tabs are set after every 8th character.
CTRL	Control Key -- used in conjunction with another key to perform a command or a function.
⇧	Shift Key -- used to change lower case letters to capitals.
ALT	Alternate Key -- used with alpha typing keys to enter BASIC keywords.
←	Backspace Key -- used to move the cursor one character to the left whenever the key is pressed.
↵	Enter Key -- used to move cursor from final character position on a line to the first position on the next line.

Illustration 4-4. IBM Keyboard (Program Function Keys)

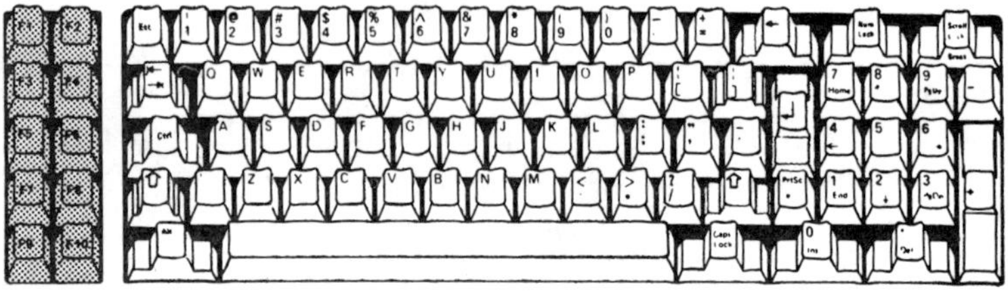

Table 4-2. Program Function Keys

Key	Explanation
F1	LIST Function -- is used to display the lines of your program on the screen.
F2	RUN Function -- is used to execute a program from its beginning.
F3	LOAD Function -- is used to read a program from a storage device (ex. cassette tape) and store it in main memory.
F4	SAVE Function -- is used to store a program on a storage device from memory.

Table 4-2. Program Function Keys (Cont.)

F5	CONT Function -- is used to restart a program after it has been temporarily interrupted by a STOP or CTRL BREAK.
F6	LPT1: Function -- is used to transfer data from the video screen to the line printer.
F7	TRON Function -- refers to trace on. This function causes the line numbers of program lines to be displayed as these lines are executed.
F8	TROFF Function -- refers to trace off. This function cancels function F7.
F9	KEY Function -- is used to change the function of the other 9 function keys.
F10	SCREEN Function -- is used to return a program to the character mode from the graphics mode and also turn off the color.

Illustration 4-5. IBM Keyboard (Numeric Keyboard Keys)

Table 4-3. Numeric Keypad Keys (NUM LOCK Key Depressed)

Key	Explanation
1-9	When the NUM LOCK key is depressed, keys 1 through 9 will be functioning.
• DEL	When the NUM LOCK key is depressed the decimal point will be used.
0 INS	When the NUM LOCK key is depressed, the zero will be used.
-	The Minus key is used with the numeric keypad.
+	The Plus key is used with the numeric keypad.

When the NUM LOCK key is released, the numeric keypad will be cancelled. The same keys outlined in Illustration 4-5 will retain different meanings which will be discussed in Table 4-4.

Table 4-4. Non-Numeric Keypad Keys (NUM LOC Key Released)

Key	Explanation
7 HOME	The Home key moves the cursor to the first character position in the top line on the screen.
8 ↑	The Up Arrow key moves the cursor up one line every time it is pressed.

Table 4-4. Non-Numeric Keypad Keys (NUM-LOCK Keys Released) (Cont.)

4 ←	The Left Arrow key moves the cursor to the left by one position every time it is pressed.
6 →	The Right Arrow key moves the cursor to the right by one position every time it is pressed.
2 ↓	The Down Arrow Key moves the cursor down by one line every time it is pressed.
1 END	The End key moves the cursor to the final character on the line.
• DEL	The DEL key deletes the character where the cursor is presently positioned.
0 INS	The Insert key is used to set the keyboard into the insert mode. In the insert mode, any data entries will be made at the current cursor postion and all data to the right of the cursor position will move to the right. The insert mode is exited by pressing the Insert key a second time.

The miscellaneous keys are outlined in gray in Illustration 4-6. These are described in Table 4-5.

Illustration 4-6. IBM Keyboard (Miscellaneous Keys)

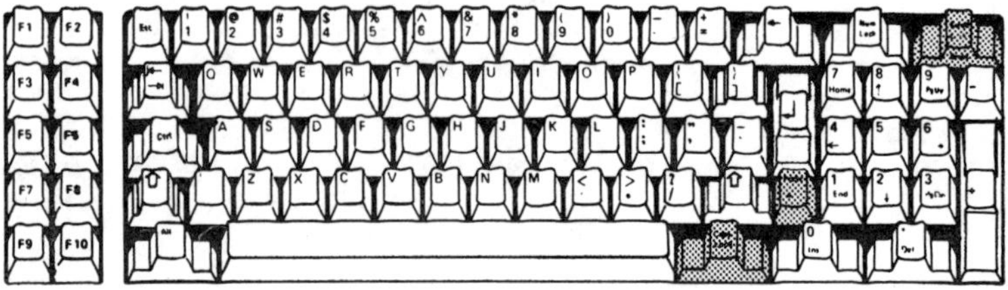

Table 4-5. Miscellaneous Keys

Key	Explanation
CAPS LOCK	Like the NUM LOCK key, the CAPS LOCK key is a toggle key. When it is depressed, the letters will be typed in capitals (upper case). When it is released, the letters will be typed in lower case.
PRT SC *	The PRT SC (or Print Screen) key prints a * with the SHIFT key released. When SHIFT is depressed, the PRT SC key will cause all data to be printed to the screen.
SCR LOCK BREAK	The SCR LOCK (Scroll Lock/Break) key is used in the unshift mode with the Control key to stop a program from running.

The Control key can be used in conjunction with other keys to create certain functions. These are listed in Table 4-6. Note that the Control key must be pressed simultaneously with the other key(s).

Table 4-6. Control Key Combinations

Control Key Combination	Explanation
CTRL + SCROLL LOCK/BREAK = BREAK	This combination can be used to stop a program while it is running, and to identify the line number where it stops.
CRTL + NUM LOCK = PAUSE	This combination is used to stop your program from running. The program will continue when any key is pressed.
CTRL +→= TAB	This combination moves the cursor to the next word on the current line.
CTRL +←= REVERSE TAB	This combination moves the cursor to the preceding word on the current line.
CTRL + HOME = CLEAR SCREEN	This combination erases all data from the screen and then moves the cursor to the upper left hand corner.
CTRL + ALT + DEL = SYSTEM RESET	If the Control and ALT keys are simultaneously pressed while the Delete key is pressed, the PC's operating system will be reloaded.

Keyboard Usage Under DOS

Some of the keys and Control key combinations have meanings specific to the IBM DOS operating system. These are listed in Table 4-7.

Table 4-7. DOS Key Usage

Key	Description
F1	This function key can be used under DOS to redisplay a line that was previously entered, one character at a time.
F2 + Character	When F2 is entered followed by a character, all of the previously entered lines will be displayed up to the first occurrence of the character following F2.
F3	This function key is used to redisplay the line previously entered.
F4 + Character	When F4 is entered followed by a character, the screen will skip all of the characters in the line previously entered up to the character entered after F4.
F5	This function key is used to save the line currently being displayed for further editing.
CTRL + NUM LOCK = SUSPEND	This combination suspends system operation so that the user can read the display. Press any key to continue operation.
CTRL + PRTSC = ECHO	This combination echos and prints whatever the user types and whatever is displayed by the system. To shut off this procedure, press CTRL + PRTSC again.
CTRL + SCR LOCK/BREAK = BREAK	This combination is used to stop your command program while it is running.

IBM Printer Operation

The IBM 80 CPS Matrix Printer will work with nearly every computer that uses a parallel interface. The IBM Printer will accept the 96 ASC II characters and symbols as well as the 64 graphic code characters. These characters can be printed in any size desired; condensed, enlarged, emphasized, and normal.

Control Switches and Lights

The various control switches and lights for the IBM Printer are shown in Illustration 4-7 and are discussed below.

Power Switch -- This switch controls the power to the printer. When it is on, the printer will be on and the power light on the control panel will be on.

Ready Light -- This light will be on when the printer is ready to receive data.

Paper Out Light -- This light will be on when the paper supply is near its end. The printer will also enact a beep as a warning.

On Line Light -- This light will be on when the power switch is first turned on.

On Line Switch -- This switch controls the on line mode. If this switch is pressed once, the printer will go to off line status, and will not be able to receive data from the computer. If the on line switch is pressed a second time, the printer will return to the on line mode.

Form Feed -- This switch can only be used when the printer is off line. When this switch is pressed, the paper will be fed to the next top-of-form position.

Top of form can be set by adjusting the form to the first print line before the printer is powered on. Once the printer has been turned on, the printer will automatically feed to the current print postion whenever the form feed switch is pressed.

Line Feed -- This switch is only active when the printer is off line. When this switch is pressed, the printer will advance the form by one line. If this switch is pressed and then held, the form will continue to advance until the switch has been released.

Illustration 4-7. IBM Printer Control Switches and Lights

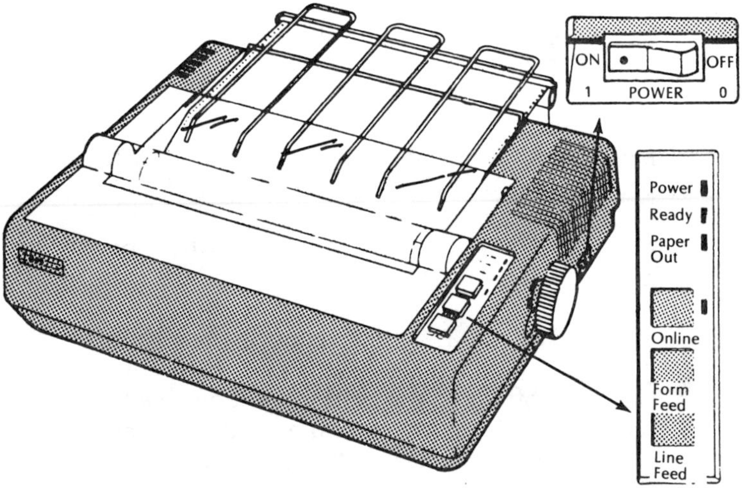

Installing The Ribbon

The installation of a ribbon in the IBM Printer is depicted in Illustrations 4-8 and 4-9. When handling the IBM ribbon cartridge, hold it by the raised handle in the center of the cartridge. This will facilitate handling and will prevent ink smudges.

Guide the two tabs on the left side of the ribbon cartridge into the two slots on the left side of the printer frame as shown in Illustration 4-8. When the cartridge is in the correct position, press it firmly into place. Turn the knob on the printer ribbon in a counterclockwise direction until any slack in the ribbon is taken up.

Finally, using either a pencil or your finger, insert the ribbon into the slot between the printhead and the ribbon shield. This is pictured in Illustration 4-9.

Installing Forms

The installation of forms in the IBM Printer is depicted in Illustrations 4-10 through 4-14. First of all, raise the printer's access cover and lift it from the base as shown in Illustration 4-10.

Be certain that your forms are properly positioned on the floor beneath your printer. The forms should be positioned behind and underneath the printer. The correct paper positioning is shown in Illustration 4-11.

Before inserting the forms in the printer, move the print scale forward, center the forms guide roller, and open the tractor covers. The location of these items is depicted in Illustration 4-12.

Illustration 4-8. IBM Printer Installation

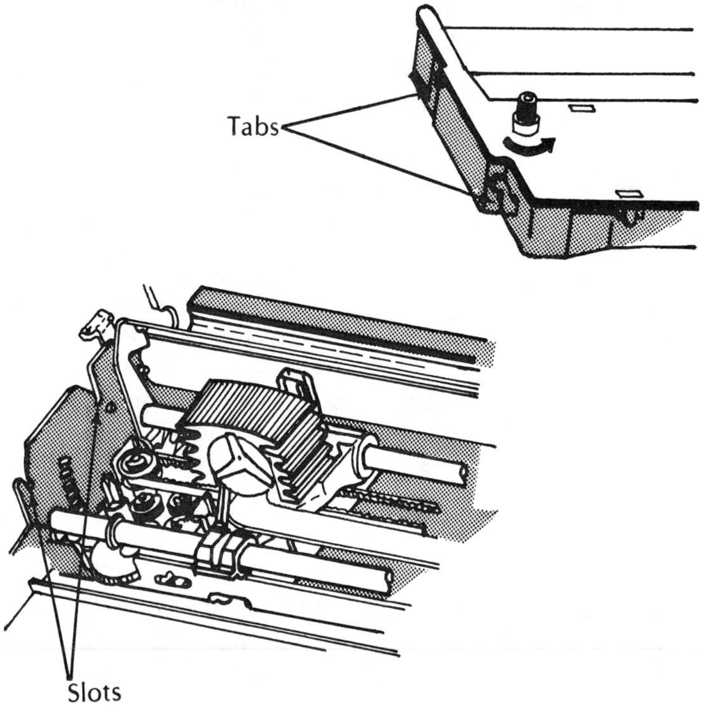

Illustration 4-9. Insertion of Ribbon Between Printhead and Ribbon Shield

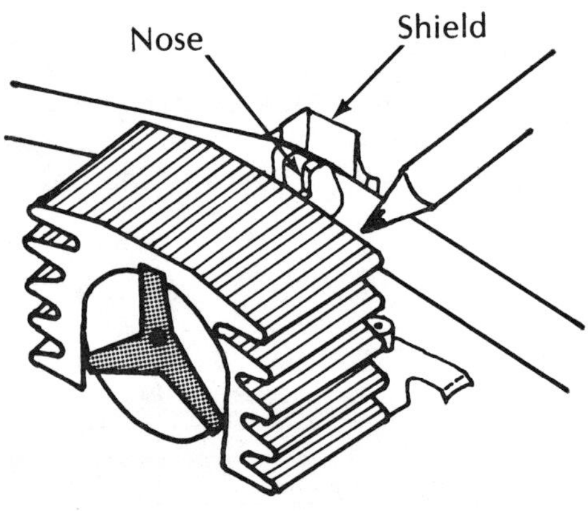

Illustration 4-10. Raising The Printer's Access Cover

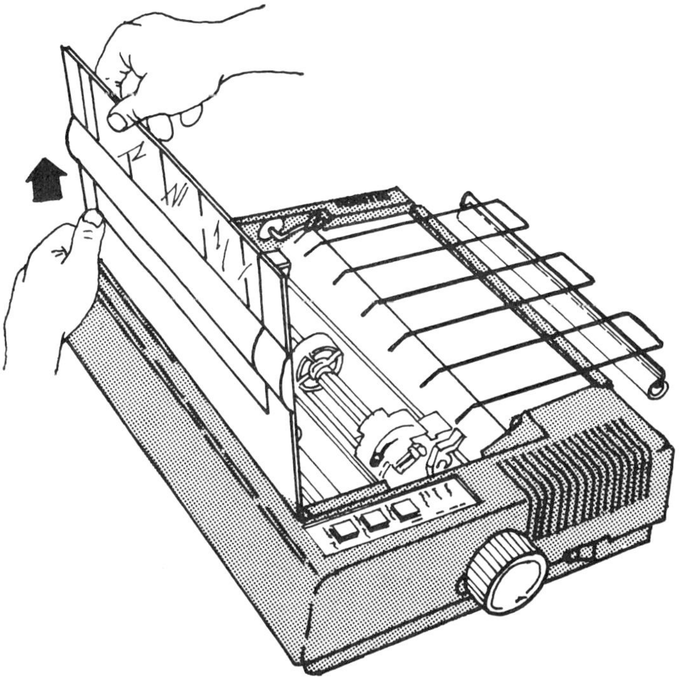

Illustration 4-11. Paper Location On The Floor

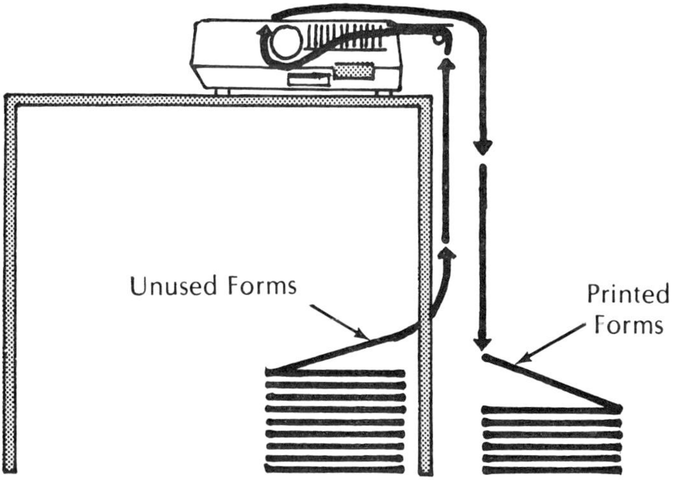

Illustration 4-12. Guiding Forms Into Printer Mechanism Opening

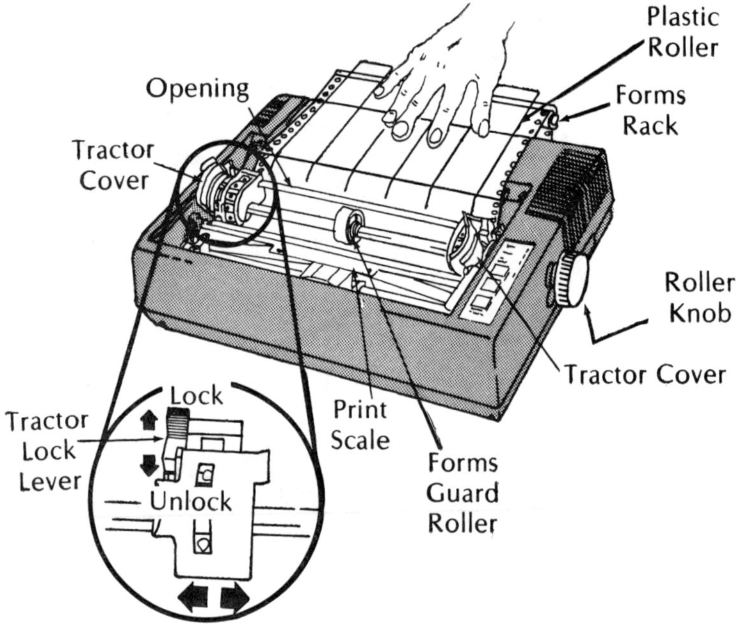

Insert the end of the forms in between the forms rack and the plastic roller and into the printer opening as shown in Illustration 4-12. Continue pushing the forms into the printer opening until a few inches of the form appears in the front of the printer.

Adjust the paper holes on the forms so they fit in the tractor pins. It may be necessary to adjust either one or both of the tractors so that the forms feed properly. Once the forms have been properly positioned in the tractor, close the tractor covers, and move the print scale up against the forms.

Be certain that the forms are feeding properly by rolling the forms forward with the roller knob located on the side of the printer. Always feed the forms forward. Never feed them backwards as this may cause damage to the printer. When you are certain that the forms are feeding properly, replace the printer access cover.

Forms Thickness Control

Your IBM printer contains a cover that allows for the adjustment of the position of the printhead to compensate for single or multi-part forms. This lever is shown in Illustration 4-13.

If you are using single part forms, move the lever toward the rear of the printer. If you are using multi-part forms, move the lever towards the front.

Left Margin Adjustment

The first step in adjusting the left print margin is to decide where you would like to have your printing start, and mark that postion on your forms. This is shown in Illustration 4-14.

Illustration 4-13. Forms Thickness Control Lever

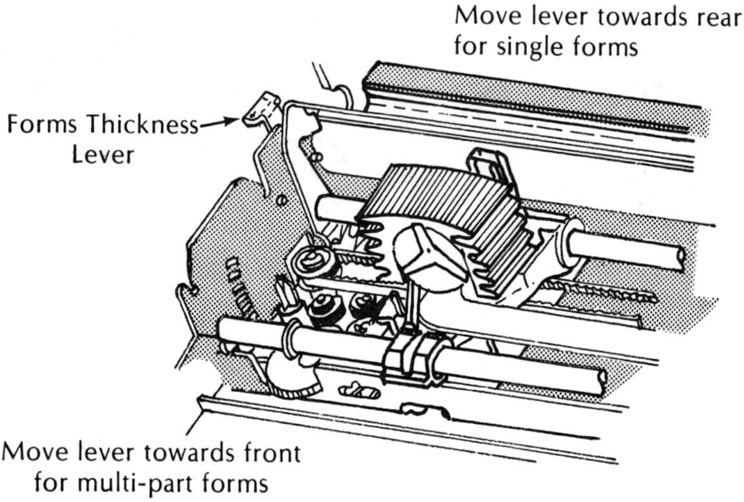

Illustration 4-14. Marking Print Position

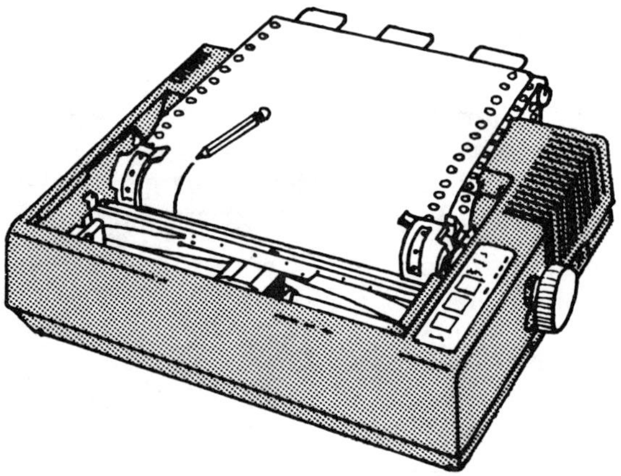

Next, release both the right and left tractor lock levers. Move both the forms and the tractor assemblies until the mark that you had previously drawn is aligned with the zero position on the print scale. This is depicted in Illustration 4-15. Then, lock the tractor assemblies back into place.

Illustration 4-15. Aligning Forms With Print Scale

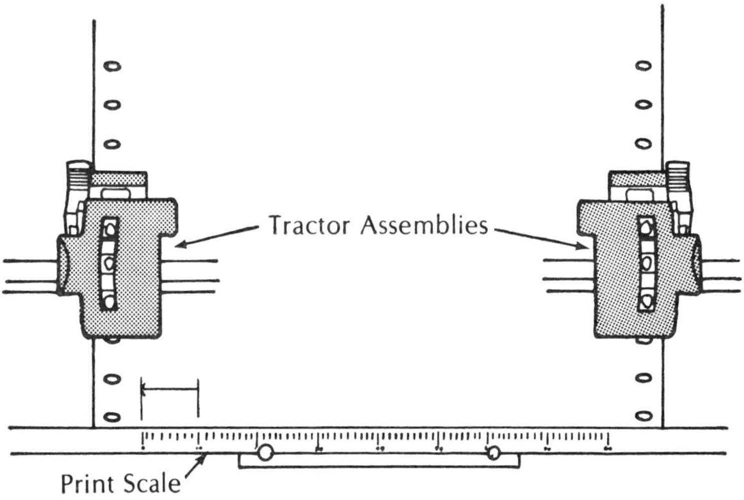

Printer Self-Test

The printer self-test is used to determine whether or not the printer is operating properly. To perform the printer self-test, first of all, turn the power switch on both the printer and the System Unit to the off position. Then, disconnect the printer cable from the System Unit.

Next, turn the printer's power switch back on, press and hold the line feed switch. Once, the printing starts, you can release the line feed switch. The complete test requires approximately ten minutes. You can stop the test any time by turning the power switch to the off position. A sample of the printer self-test output is shown in Illustration 4-16.

Illustration 4-16. Printer Self-Test Output Sample

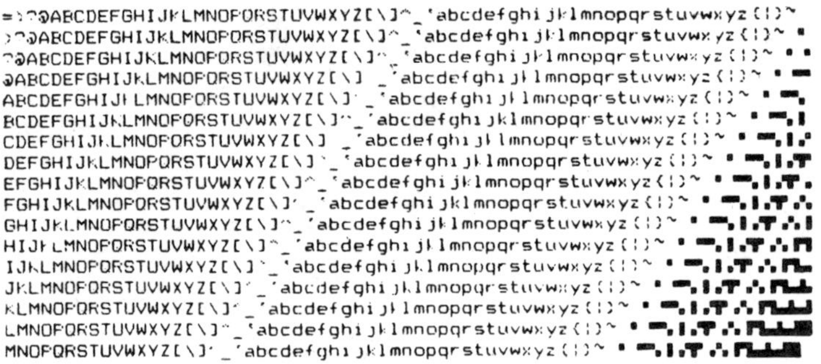

IBM Printer ASC II Codes

Data to be printed is communicated to the printer via the System Unit. In Illustrations 4-17, 4-18, and 4-19, you will find the ASC II codes used to represent the various symbols, characters, and graphics output by the printer.

There are certain special characters known as ASC II control codes which determine in what manner characters are output on the printer. For example, control characters can be used to print characters at double width, at a compressed width, or in an emphasized fashion. The various ASC II Control Characters used by the IBM Printer are shown in Table 4-8.

The ASC II Control Codes are sent to the printer via the LPRINT and CHR$ commands in Microsoft Basic. For example, the following statement:

LPRINT CHR$ (14); "John Doe"

will print John Doe in the double width mode.

Some of the ASC II control characters must be preceded by the ASC II code for NUL (128). In Table 4-8, the ASC II control characters that should be preceded with 128 are identified with an asterisk. The following BASIC command would set the printer so that the double strike mode would be turned on.

LPRINT CHR$ (128) + CHR$ (71)

Other ASC II Control Characters must be preceded by the ASC II code for Escape (27). These are identified in Table 4-8 by a double asterisk. The following BASIC command would set the printer so that the double width mode would be turned off:

LPRINT CHR$ (27) + CHR$ (20)

Table 4-8. ASC II Control Codes

ASC II	Control Code Description
0**	NULL. Should follow ESC "B" and ESC "D" to cancel TAB's.
0*	Used to set line spacing to 1/8". Should follow ESC "A".
1*	Sets line spacing to 7/72". Again, follows ESC "A".
2*	Returns the line spacing to the amount set earlier by ESC "A". The default value is 1/6" spacing.
7	Sounds the buzzer for 3½ seconds.
10*	Line Feed Character (LF)
11**	Vertical Tab (VT).
12**	Advances forms to next top-of-form (TF).

Table 4-8. ASC II Control Codes (Cont.)

13*	Carriage Return.
14	Turns on Double Width Mode (SO).
15	Turns on Compressed Character (SI).
17**	Selects printer -- allowing it to accept data (DC1).
18**	Shuts off Compressed Character Mode (DC2).
19**	Deselects printer--not allowing it to accept data (DC3).
20**	Shuts off Double Width Mode (DC4).
24**	CANCELS unprinted Data. Resets Double Width and Compressed Character to normal width.
27	Escape code.
65*	ASC II "A" Code. Sets spacing of Line Feed (LF) with 0, 1, or 2.
66*	ASC II "B" code. Sets Vertical Tabs (VT) up to 64.
67*	ASC II "C" code. Sets Form Length (FL). Default value is 66.
68*	ASC II "D" code. Sets Horizontal Tabs (HT) up to 80 (or 132).
69*	ASC II "E" code. Turns on Emphasized mode.

Table 4-8. ASC II Control Codes (Cont.)

70*	ASC II "F" code. Turns off Emphasized mode.
71*	ASC II "G" code. Turns on Double Strike Mode.
72*	ASC II "H" code. Turns off Double Strike Mode.
127	Deletes any Data not printed. Resets Double Width and Compressed Characters to normal.

Illustration 4-17. ASC II Character, Symbol, and Graphics Codes

Characters & Symbols — **Graphics**

NUL 0	16	SP 32	Ø 48	@ 64	P 80	96	p 112	NUL 128	144	160	176	192	208
1	DC1 17	! 33	1 49	A 65	Q 81	a 97	q 113	129	DC1 145	161	177	193	209
2	18	34	2 50	B 66	R 82	b 98	r 114	130	146	162	178	194	210
3	DC3 19	# 35	3 51	C 67	S 83	c 99	s 115	131	DC3 147	163	179	195	211
4	DC4 20	$ 36	4 52	D 68	T 84	d 100	t 116	132	DC4 148	164	180	196	212
5	21	% 37	5 53	E 69	U 85	e 101	u 117	133	149	165	181	197	213
6	22	& 38	6 54	F 70	V 86	f 102	v 118	134	150	166	182	198	214
BEL 7	23	39	7 55	G 71	W 87	g 103	w 119	BEL 135	151	167	183	199	215
8	CAN 24	(40	8 56	H 72	X 88	h 104	x 120	136	CAN 152	168	184	200	216
HT 9	25	) 41	9 57	I 73	Y 89	i 105	y 121	HT 137	153	169	185	201	217
LF 10	26	* 42	58	J 74	Z 90	j 106	z 122	LF 138	154	170	186	202	218
VT 11	ESC 27	+ 43	59	K 75	[91	k 107	123	VT 139	ESC 155	171	187	203	219
FF 12	28	44	< 60	L 76	\ 92	l 108	124	FF 140	156	172	188	204	220
CR 13	29	- 45	= 61	M 77	] 93	m 109	125	CR 141	157	173	189	205	221
SO 14	30	. 46	> 62	N 78	^ 94	n 110	~ 126	SO 142	158	174	190	206	222
SI 15	31	/ 47	? 63	O 79	_ 95	o 111	DEL 127	SI 143	159	175	191	207	223

Illustration 4-18. ASC II Character and Symbol Matrix with ASC II Numbers

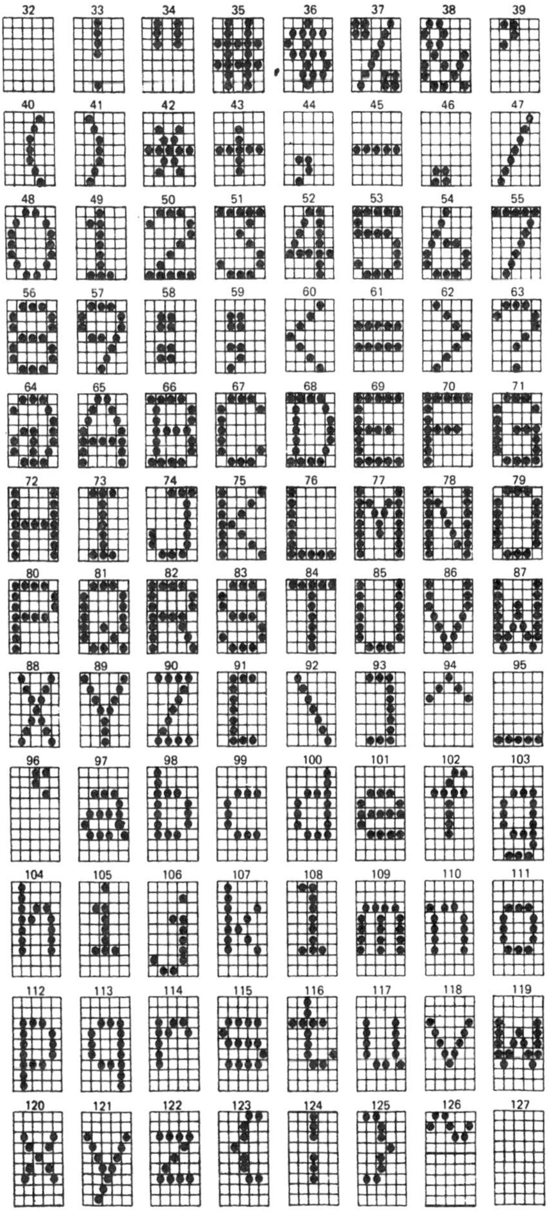

Illustration 4-19. Graphics Matrix with ASC II Numbers

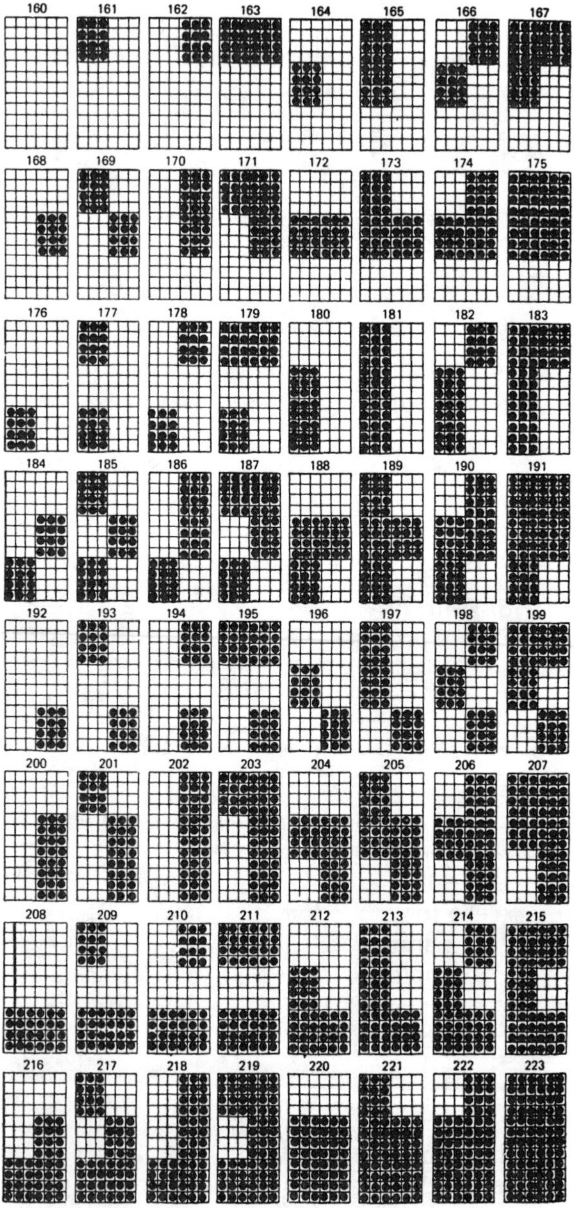

Chapter 5. Using IBM DOS

Introduction

DOS is an abbreviation for Disk Operating System. IBM DOS consists of a group of programs which allows the user to manage information on diskette.

The DOS programs are themselves provided on a diskette known as the DOS diskette. You should not use your original DOS diskette in day to day operations -- use copies instead.

You will learn how to copy your DOS diskette in this chapter. You will also learn how to start up DOS and how the most often used DOS commands are implemented.

Notice that your DOS diskette does not have a write protect notch. If a diskette does not have a write protect notch, it is permanently write protected and no data can be written to it by the computer. This will prevent the user from accidentally erasing data by overwriting it with new data.

Notation

DOS allows the user to enter data with uppercase letters, lowercase letters, or a combination of both. To prevent confusion, we will use upper and lowercase letters in our examples except for the names of DOS commands, program names, and file names. These will be displayed in uppercase letters in our examples.

Starting DOS

Generally, you will want to start or load DOS whenever you start your PC. When you start (or load) DOS, a copy of the DOS programs are read from the DOS diskette and loaded into the computer's memory. The diskette drive will emit a series of noises while the DOS programs are being read from the DOS diskette and loaded into memory.

The steps involved in loading DOS with the computer off are as follows:

1. Insert DOS diskette in drive A and close diskette door.

2. Turn on printer, monitor and then computer.

3. A pause of 3 to 45 seconds will occur while the system check takes place. The diskette drive will emit a series of noises while DOS is being read into memory.

If the computer is already on, use the following steps to load DOS.

1. Insert the DOS diskette in drive A and close the drive door.

2. Press the CTRL and ALT keys, and while holding them, press DEL. Then, release all three.

3. The diskette drive's in use light will come on while DOS is being read into memory.

This procedure is known as the system reset, and can be used while running your computer to restart DOS.

Entering The Date

When DOS has been loaded and is ready, a message similar to that shown below will be displayed on the screen.

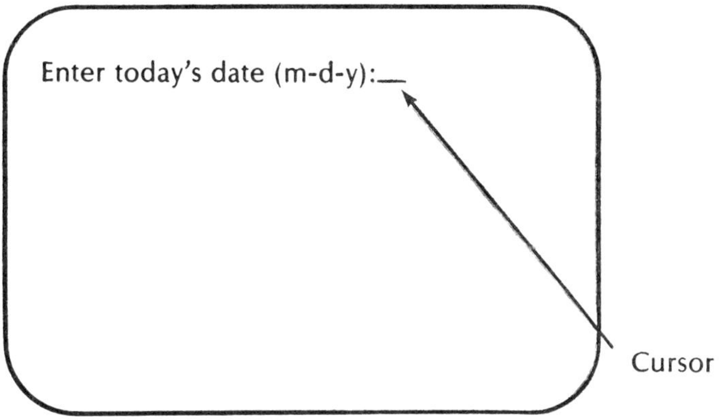

You should enter the current date as follows:

1. Enter one or two numbers from 1 to 12 for the month.
2. Enter a dash (-) or a slash (/).
3. Enter one or two numbers from 1 to 31 for the day.
4. Enter a second dash or slash.
5. Enter two numbers between 80 and 99 for the year.
6. Press the Enter key.

DOS will check the date that you entered to be certain that it is a valid entry. If not, the following will be displayed.

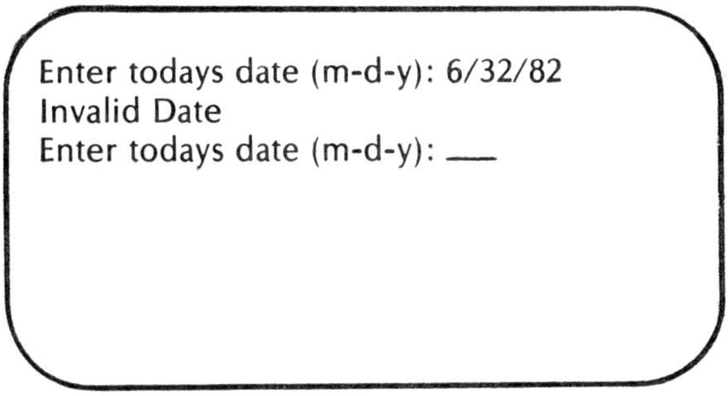

DOS Prompt

Once a valid date has been entered, the following will be displayed on your screen.

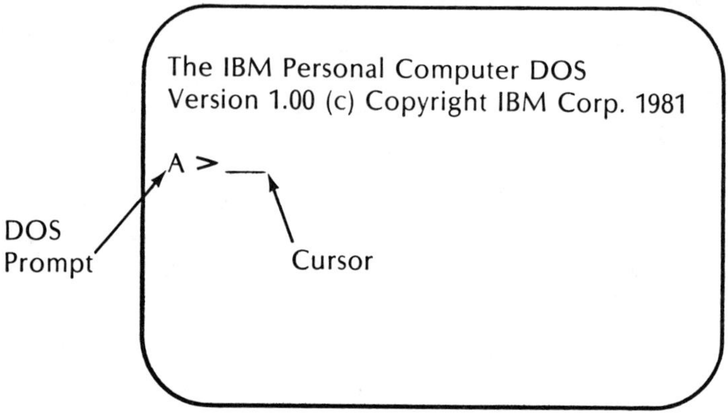

A > is known as the DOS **prompt**. A prompt is an indication to the user that he is to enter data. Another prompt that you will encounter is the BASIC prompt, Ok. This prompt signals the user that he is to respond with a BASIC command.

The initial position of the DOS prompt is a letter (A or B). This letter identifies which drive is the default drive (or current drive). The default drive is the drive that DOS supposes will contain the diskette or files specified by your commands.

You can change the default drive from A to B by entering the following:

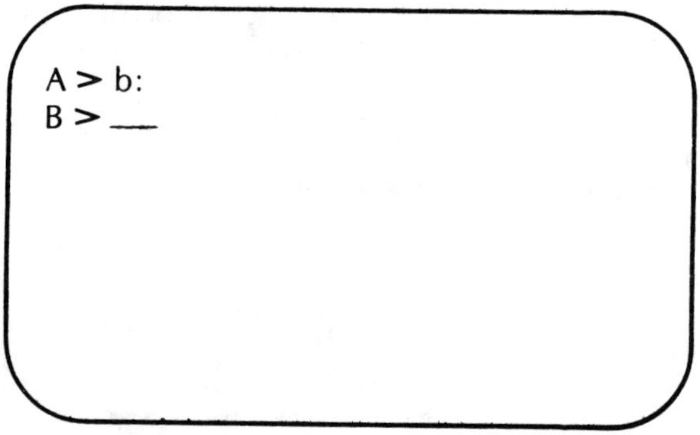

When B is the default drive, DOS will look to the diskette in drive B whenever a file is specified without a **drive identifier.**

The drive identifier consists of the drive letter and a colon preceding the filename (ex: B:TEXT.DAT).

DOS Keyboard Usage

In the next few pages, we will discuss how some of the keys on the IBM keyboard are used with DOS.

Entering A Command

The Enter key is used to execute or start a command after it has been typed in.

Stopping A Command

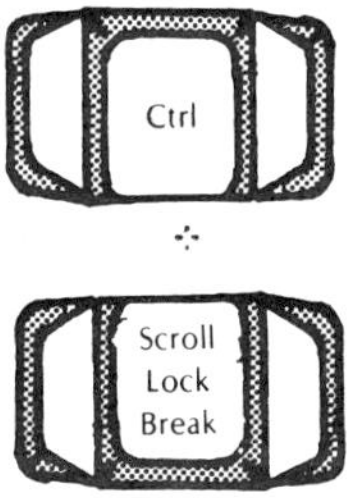

A command can be stopped by pressing and holding the control key while pressing the break key. When both keys are released, the command will stop. The DOS prompt will appear, and the next command can be entered.

Correcting Typing Errors

There are several ways of correcting errors in DOS commands. We will discuss two of the most commonly used here, the Backspace and the Escape keys. Note that mistakes can only be corrected before the Enter key is pressed to execute the command.

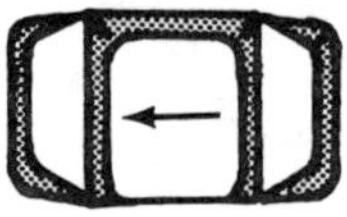

The Backspace key moves the cursor one character to the left. The Backspace key deletes characters as the cursor is moved to the left. Once the Backspace key has been used to erase the erroneous characters, the correct characters can be entered.

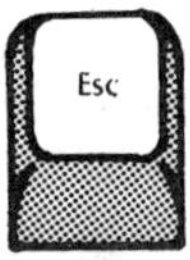

The Escape key can be used to erase an entire line. A backslash will appear, and the cursor will move down one line on the screen where the command can be re-entered.

Slow Screen Scrolling

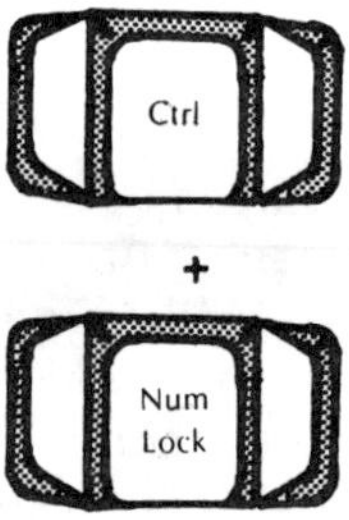

Scrolling is a term which is used to describe the process where information continues to move upward on the screen as new information replaces it on the bottom of the screen.

If scrolling is taking place too fast for you to read the data on the screen, press the Control and Num Lock keys together and then release them. To display new data, press any key.

Send Data on the Screen to the Printer

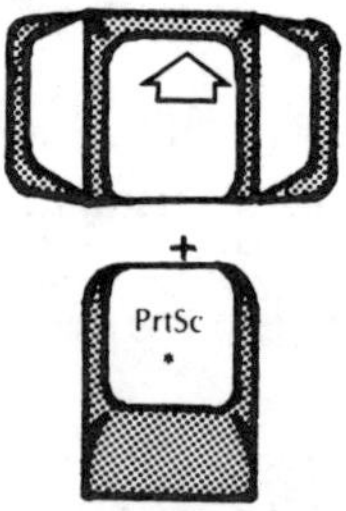

You may wish to send the data appearing on the screen to the printer as well. First of all, be sure that your printer is turned on and loaded with paper. Then, press and hold either of the shift keys while pressing the Prtsc (Print Screen) key.

System Reset

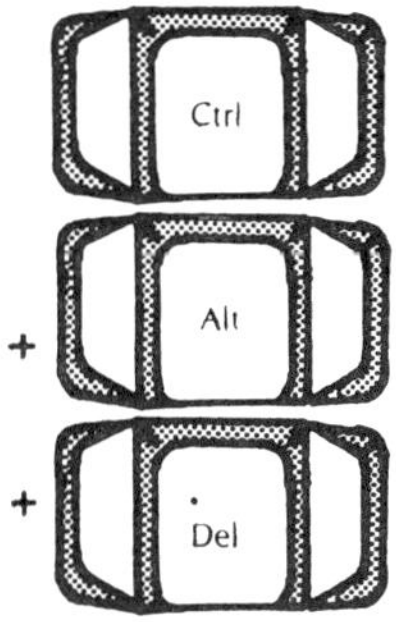

As previously mentioned, if you wish to begin DOS over again, be sure a DOS diskette is in drive A and then press and hold the Ctrl and Alt keys and press the Del key. Then, release all three keys. DOS will be reloaded and the DOS startup message will appear.

Copying Your DOS Diskette

As mentioned previously, you should make a copy of the DOS diskette that is supplied with your IBM PC. This original DOS diskette is also known as the **master diskette**.

You should use your copies or **back-ups** in day-to-day operation, and store your master diskette in a safe place. That way, if your back-up DOS diskette becomes damaged or misplaced, you can make additional copies from your master.

Copying The DOS Diskette With One Drive

If you have only one disk drive with your IBM Personal Computer, follow the procedures in this section.

Step 1. Start DOS and be certain the DOS prompt (A >) is displayed.

Step 2. Enter the following:

```
A > format a:
```

The following message will be displayed.

```
A> format a:

Insert new diskette for drive A
and strike any key when ready.
```

Be certain that you do not touch the keyboard until the DOS diskette has been removed.

Step 3. Remove the DOS diskette and insert a blank diskette. Press any key to begin the formatting process. The message, formatting, will be displayed as the formatting takes place. After the formatting process has been completed, the following will be displayed.

```
Formatting . . . Format complete
Format another (Y/N)? __
```

Enter n to indicate that you do not wish to format another diskette. You need not press Enter after typing n.

The DOS prompt will appear on the screen.

Step 4. Remove the newly formatted diskette from the drive and insert the DOS diskette in its place. Enter the following:

```
A > diskcopy
```

Step 5. After the previous entry, the following will appear:

```
Insert source diskette in drive A
Strike any key when ready
```

With the DOS diskette in drive A, press any key.

Step 6. The following message will be displayed.

```
Insert target diskette in drive A
Strike any key when ready
```

Before pressing a key, be certain that you have removed the DOS diskette (source diskette) and have inserted the recently formatted blank diskette (target diskette). After this has been completed, press any key.

Step 7. Wait a few seconds, and the following message will be displayed.

```
Insert source diskette in drive A
Strike any key when ready
```

When this message appears, remove the back-up diskette from the disk drive and insert the DOS diskette. When the DOS diskette has been inserted, press any key to continue.

Step 8. Continue repeating Steps 6 and 7 until the following message appears on the screen.

```
Copy complete
Copy another? (Y/N)
```

At this point, type n. You need not press the Enter key.

Step 9. Next type the following:

diskcomp

and then press the Enter key. The following message will be displayed.

```
Insert first diskette in drive A
Strike any key when ready
```

Press any key.

Step 10. The following message will now appear.

```
Insert second diskette in drive A.
Strike any key when ready
```

Remove the DOS diskette and insert the back-up diskette. Press any key.

Step 11. The following message will now appear.

```
Insert first diskette in drive A
Strike any key when ready
```

Remove the back-up diskette, insert the DOS diskette, and press any key.

Step 12. Continue repeating Steps 10 and 11 until the following message is displayed.

```
Diskettes compare ok
Compare more diskettes? (Y/N)
```

Enter n in reponse to this prompt. The DOS prompt (A >) will then be displayed.

Remove the DOS back-up diskette from the drive and label* it properly. Store your master DOS diskette in a secure location.

*Always use a felt-tip pen to label a diskette. Never use a ball-point pen or pencil.

Copying The DOS Diskette With Two Drives

Step 1. First of all, be sure that DOS has been loaded and that the DOS prompt (A >) appears on your screen. Your master DOS diskette should be inserted in drive A.

Step 2. Insert the back-up diskette into drive B, and type the following:

```
format b:
```

and press Enter.

The following message will be displayed.

```
Insert new diskette for drive B:
and strike any key when ready.
```

Press any key.

Step 3. The following message will be displayed as the diskette in drive B is being formatted.

```
Formatting . . .
```

After the formatting process has been completed, the following message will be displayed.

```
Formatting . . . Format complete
Format another (Y/N)? __
```

Enter the following:

n

You need not press Enter.

Step 4. The DOS prompt (A >) will appear. You are now ready to copy DOS to the newly formatted diskette in drive B.

Type the following:

diskcopy a: b:

and press Enter. The following message will appear.

```
Insert source diskette in drive A
Insert target diskette in drive B
Strike any key when ready
```

Since the DOS diskette was already inserted in drive A, and the target diskette in drive B, you can strike any key to begin the copying process. The in use light will go on and off on both drives as DOS is read from the diskette in drive A and copied onto the diskette in drive B.

Step 5. When the copying process has been completed, the following message will be displayed.

```
Copy complete
Copy another? (Y/N) __
```

Enter n and the DOS prompt (A >) will be displayed.

Step 6. Enter the following command to be certain that the copy in drive B is the same as the master DOS diskette in drive A.

```
diskcomp a: b:
```

The following message will be displayed.

```
Insert first diskette in drive A
Insert second diskette in drive B
Strike any key when ready
```

Step 7. The disk drive in use lights will blink on and off as the two diskettes are compared. When the comparison has been completed, the following message will be displayed.

```
Diskettes compare ok
Compare more diskettes? (Y/N)
```

Enter n and remove both diskettes. Use a felt-tip pen to label the back-up diskette.

Files, Filenames and Filename Match Characters

At this point, you have gained some knowledge as to the organization of diskettes (Chapter 1). You have gained an introductory knowledge of DOS and have learned how to copy your DOS diskette master. Before continuing our discussion of DOS, we will explain the concepts of files, filenames, and filename extensions.

A file is a group of related information. For example, a file might consist of a list of all the names, addresses, and phone numbers of your customers. A file might also contain the text of a standard form letter you send to sales prospects. A file could also contain a program to edit and print the form letters.

The advantage of grouping information in a file is that it can be easily retrieved by DOS, and can be stored on diskette when it is not being used.

A number of files can be stored on a single diskette. IBM DOS allows up to 64 files per diskette. Every file that is stored on the same diskette must have a unique filename. In other words, no two files on the same diskette can have the same filename.

A filename consists of a primary filename and an optional filename extension. Examples of filenames are given below.

TEXT.DAT
PROGRAM1
NEW.TXT
ACCOUNT.BAS

Note that example 2 does not contain a filename extension.

IBM DOS allows primary filenames of up to eight characters in length. These characters can be the letters of the alphabet, integer numbers (0-9), or the following symbols:

$ # & @ ! % ( ) - { } <>‘ _ \ ^ ~ | ’

The filename extension is an optional name that can appear after the primary filename. The filename extension begins with a period and either one, two, or three characters. When a filename extension is included in a filename, both the primary filename and the extension must be used to identify the file in DOS.

When inventing filenames, it is a good idea to make up a filename that somehow identifies the information contained in that program. For example:

CUSTLIST.BAS

would be a good name for a BASIC program file that printed a list of your firm's customers.

When a filename is given in DOS, more information than merely the filename is required. DOS also needs to know where the file can be found. This is accomplished through the use of a **drive specifer**.

A drive specifier consists of a letter and a colon (ex. A:) that proceeds the filename. The letter identifies the drive where the file can be found. The filename and the drive specifier when taken together are known as the **file specifier**.

In many cases, you will not be required to include the drive specifier. When the drive specifer is the same as the current or default drive, the drive specifier need not be entered.

For example, if the default drive is A (the prompt will be A>), either of the following could be used to identify CUSTLIST.BAS to DOS.

a:custlist.bas   or   custlist.bas

In certain situations, you may wish to perform the same DOS operations with several files. For example, you might wish to copy all of the data files on one diskette to another diskette. DOS includes two **filename match** characters. These allow the user to specify a number of files with just one specification. These characters are the asterisk (*) and the question mark (?).

The question mark when used as a filename match character in a primary filename or a filename extension means that any character can be in that position.

For example, if the current drive (A) contained the following files:

TEXT1.DAT
TEXT2.DAT
TEXT3.DAT
TEXT4.DAT
TEXT5.BAK

and the following DOS command was entered:

dir text?.dat

All files except TEXT5.BAK would be listed.

If the following DOS command was entered:

dir text?.???

all of the above files would be listed.

The asterisk (*) in a primary filename is used to indicate that any character can be placed in that particular position and in the rest of the filename. The asterisk can also be used in a filename extension to indicate that any character can be placed in that position and in the remainder of the filename extension.

Using our previous example's files, if the following DOS command were entered:

dir *.bak

The following file would be listed.

text5.bak

If the following DOS command were entered:

dir text?.*

all of the files would be listed.

DOS Files

The following files are on your DOS diskette and can be listed with the directory command.

COMMAND	.COM	DANDY	.BAS
CHKDSK	.COM	HAT	.BAS
SYS	.COM	SAMPLES	.BAS
FORMAT	.COM	BUG	.BAS
TIME	.COM	DONKEY	.BAS
DATE	.COM	POP	.BAS
DEBUG	.COM	MARCH	.BAS
EDLIN	.COM	SCALES	.BAS
DISKCOMP	.COM	MORTGAGE	.BAS
DISKCOPY	.COM	CALENDAR	.BAS
MODE	.COM	BLUE	.BAS
COMP	.COM	FORTY	.BAS
LINK	.EXE	STARS	.BAS
BASIC	.COM	SAKURA	.BAS
BASICA	.COM	CIRCLE	.BAS
ART	.BAS	PIECHART	.BAS
COLORBAR	.BAS	BALL	.BAS
MUSIC	.BAS	COMM	.BAS
HUMOR	.BAS	SPACE	.BAS

The following two files are contained on your DOS diskette, but they will not appear on a directory listing.

IBMBIO.COM
IBMDOS.COM

These files form the core of any diskette containing DOS. They use up 2 of the 64 possible files that can be included on a diskette.

Resident Commands

Most of the DOS commands are in fact programs contained on the DOS diskette. However, a few of the more commonly used commands are known as **resident** commands. These commands are stored in the computer's memory and are available as needed by the user. The following DOS commands are resident commands.

COPY
DIR
ERASE
RENAME
TYPE

Formatting A Diskette

Before using a new diskette, you must format it using the FORMAT command (see Chapter 6). The FORMAT command writes on every sector of your diskette, initializes the **directory**, initializes the **File Allocation Table**, and places a program known as the **boot record** at the beginning of your diskette.

The directory is used to store the names of the files on your diskette along with other data regarding the files such as size, location, and date created.

The File Allocation Table is located adjacent to the directory on the diskette. The File Allocation Table keeps track of which sectors belong to which file, and also of the available unused disk space.

Each diskette contains one directory and two copies of the File Allocation Table. The second copy is used as insurance in case the first is unreadable for some reason.

Backing Up Diskettes

You should always make back-up copies of your important diskettes, so if a diskette becomes damaged or a file is accidentally erased, you will still have access to that information. IBM DOS includes two different commands for creating back-ups; DISKCOPY and COPY.

The DISKCOPY command is used to copy an entire diskette to another. DISKCOPY copies every file on the diskette including DOS in one operation. DISKCOPY is the fastest method of copying a diskette.

DISKCOPY is only recommended when copying to new diskettes (formatted). If the diskette being copied to either has defective tracks or has had a large amount of data written and then erased, the use of the COPY command is recommended.

The COPY command can also be used to copy one or more of a diskette's files to a different diskette. The COPY command is slower than the DISKCOPY command. However, it is the preferable method of copying to a diskette where a substantial amount of data writing and erasure had taken place. This is because unlike the DISKCOPY command which creates an exact duplicate of the original, the COPY command writes files sequentially -- or one right after the other. This sequential writing of files results in better performance as the files are all grouped together. When files are copied with DISKCOPY, they may be spread throughout the diskette.

DOS Components

The core of DOS consists of three programs; the boot record, IBMBIO.COM, and IBMDOS.COM.

The boot record is a program that lies at the very beginning of your DOS diskette. The boot record is automatically loaded into memory when DOS is started (or booted). The boot record then loads the remaining DOS programs. The boot record is placed on all diskettes by the FORMAT program.

IBMBIO.COM is a program which handles the transfer of data between the computer's memory and the various input and output devices attached to it. IBMBIO.COM is also placed on the diskette by the FORMAT program. IBMBIO.COM will not be included in a directory listing of a DOS diskette's files.

IBMDOS.COM includes a file management program and a number of service programs that are used to control programs written to run under DOS. Like IBMBIO.COM, IBMDOS.COM will not be included in a directory listing of a DOS diskette's files.

Chapter 6. DOS Reference Guide

Introduction

In this chapter, we will explain each of the DOS commands except EDLIN, LINK, and DEBUG which will be discussed in Chapter 7.

IBM DOS commands can either be internal commands or external commands. Internal commands are stored in memory and therefore can be executed immediately. External commands are stored on the diskette as program files, and must be read from the diskette before they can be executed.

Any file with the filename extension, .COM or .EXE, is regarded by DOS as an external command. When entering an external command, you should not include the filename extension.

DOS Command Format

In this chapter, we will use a standardized format to explain the usage of the DOS commands. The following standards will be followed.

1. All keywords (or reserved words) will be noted in capital letters. Keywords or reserved words are words that have a predefined meaning to the system.

2. Any optional entries to be made by the user are specified in lower case italics.

3. Items enclosed by brackets [ ] are optional entries.

4. An ellipsis (. . .) indicates that an item may be repeated as desired.

5. All punctuation marks (. , : etc.) must be entered in the position specified.

6. All drive specifiers will be identified with the following:

d:

The user can enter either A: or B: in place of *d:*. If the drive specifier is not included, the current or default drive will be assumed.

7. All filenames that can be supplied by the user will be identified with the following:

filename

Only valid filenames can be entered.

8. Certain devices have been assigned reserved names. In certain commands, these can be used in place of filenames. These include the following:

CON: This identifies the console device i.e. the keyboard and video screen.

AUX: or COM1: This identifies the first Asynchronous Communications Adapter port.

LPT1: or PRN: This identifies the printer.

NUL: This is used to identify a dummy device which can be used for testing.

9. When you are specifying a filename that must be used with an extension, be certain that the extension is included in your command. Otherwise, the file specified will not be found. Filename extensions will be identified as follows:

.ext

Filename extensions consist of one to three characters preceded with a period.

10. When a filename, its extension, and a drive identifier are used together, this combination is referred to as a file specification. In this chapter, we will use the following to reference file specifications:

filespec

Examples of file specifications include the following:

b:TEXT.DAT
A:PROGRAM
NEWPROG.BAS

Note that both the drive identifier and the filename extension are optional.

Using CON: As An Input Device

The CON: device is often used to input data into a file. When CON: is used as an input device, the F6 key followed by Enter is used to mark the end-of-file. This also indicates the end of the use of CON: as an input device.

Commands and Parameters

In the remainder of this chapter, we will present individual explanations of the various DOS commands.

A DOS command generally consists of two parts; the command's reserved word (ex. COPY, DATE) followed by the command parameter (ex. a:file.txt; b:new.txt). When put together, the command and parameter appear as in the following example.

COPY a:file.txt b:new.txt

Note that commands and parameters are separated by blank spaces, colons, semi-colons, equal signs, and tab keys. These separators are known as **delimiters.** Be certain that the delimiters are properly inserted in your DOS commands, or errors will result.

BATCH PROCESSING

Type: Internal

Batch processing allows automatic execution of a file with a filename extension of .BAT. Naturally, this file must have been created before it can be executed as a batch file.

Configuration

[*d:*] *filename* [*parameters*]

Notice that only the primary filename and not the filename extension (.BAT) need be entered. The .BAT extension is assumed.

You can temporarily stop batch processing by pressing the Ctrl and Break keys. When these keys are pressed, the following prompt will appear.

Terminate batch job (Y/N)?

If Y is entered, batch processing will be ended and the system prompt (A >) will appear. If N is entered, the current command only will be ended, and batch processing will continue with the next command in the file.

AUTOEXEC.BAT File

The AUTOEXEC.BAT file represents a special use of batch processing. Whenever DOS is started, the command processor searches for the AUTOEXEC.BAT file. If this file is present, it will be executed automatically upon system start-up.

If AUTOEXEC is used, DOS will not prompt for the date -- unless the DATE command is included in the AUTOEXEC.BAT file.

Creating A Batch File

A batch file can be created either via the line editor (EDLIN) or by using the console as an input device. The line editor will be explained later in this chapter. We will explain the use of the console here.

Suppose that you wished to create an AUTOEXEC.BAT file that would automatically run a BASIC program called LIST.BAS. Your first entry would be as follows:

A > COPY CON: AUTOEXEC.BAT

The preceding command instructs DOS to copy from the console device into AUTOEXEC.BAT. Your next entry would be as follows:

BASIC LIST

This preceding entry places a command in AUTOEXEC.BAT to load BASIC and run the LIST program.

Press the F6 key followed by Enter to mark the end of the AUTOEXEC.BAT file and end the use of CON: for input. Now, when DOS is started, BASIC will automatically be loaded and LIST.BAS will be run.

Using Replaceable Parameters With .BAT Files

When you enter the commands to be included in a batch file, you can include **replaceable parameters.** These replaceable parameters will be replaced by values specified when the batch-file is executed.

Up to 9 replaceable parameters can be used. These are %0, %1, %2, %3, %4, %5, %6, %7, %8, and %9. The dummy parameters are replaced one by one in ascending order. The first dummy parameter, %0, is always replaced by the filename of the batch file preceded by the drive designator (if one is specified).

The following entries illustrate the use of replaceable parameters in a batch file.

```
A > Copy CON: FILE.BAT
Copy %1.TXT %2.TXT
Type %2.TXT
Type %0.BAT
[1]F6
1 File copied
A>
```

The batch file named FILE.BAT will now be placed on the diskette in the current drive, A.

Executing A Batch File With Replaceable Parameters

To execute a batch file with replaceable parameters, simply enter the name of the batch file followed by the parameters to be substituted for %1, %2, %3 etc.

If the following were entered:

FILE.BAT A:OLD B:NEW

FILE is substituted for 0%, A:OLD is substituted for 1%, and B:NEW is substituted for 2%.

[1]F6 indicates that the F6 key is to be pressed.

CHKDSK

Type: External

CHKDSK is also known as the Check Disk command. The Check Disk command is used to check on a diskette and report on its status.

Configuration

CHKDSK [*d:*]

After the diskette has been checked, any pertinent error messages will be displayed along with the following status report:

```
A > CHKDSK

     xx  disk files
 xxxxxx  bytes total disk space
 xxxxxx  bytes remain available

xxxxxxx  bytes total memory
xxxxxxx  bytes free
```

The X's will be replaced by integers in an actual display.

It is recommended that you periodically run CHKDSK on your frequently used diskettes to check for errors and determine available free space.

COMP

Type: External

The COMP or Compare command is used to compare the contents of two files.

Configuration

COMP [*filespec*][*d:*][*filename*[*.ext*]]

You need not specify the files to be compared in the command. However, if you do not, you will be prompted for these.

COMP compares the files byte by byte. If two bytes are unequal, the following will be displayed:

```
Compare error at offset xxxxxxxx
File 1 = xx
File 2 = xx
```

The first line gives the offset (in hexadecimal notation) into the file where the unequal comparison occurred. The hex values of each byte are displayed on the next two lines.

If ten errors are encountered, the COMP command will end with the following message:

10 Mismatches - aborting complete

If the files do compare with no errors, the following message will be displayed.

Enter primary filename
Or strike the Enter key to end

If you wish to end COMP, press Enter. If you wish to compare two more files, enter the file specification for the first file. The file specification will then be prompted for the second file.

COPY

Type: Internal

The Copy command is used to copy files.

Configuration

Copy *filespec* [*d:*] [*filename* [*.ext*]]

The file being copied is the first file named. If an optional second filename is given, that is the filename to be given to the file being copied. If no second filename is given, the copy file will be assigned the same filename as the original.

If you are copying a file on the same diskette; you will be required to specify a new filename. If you are copying a file to a different diskette, you will be allowed to use the same filename.

The filename match characters (? and *) can be used in the filename of both the original and the copy file.

Examples

A > COPY B:TEXT.DAT

A > COPY A:*.DAT B:

A > COPY PROGRAM.BAS B:*.BAK

A > COPY TEXT.DAT CON:

In the first example, TEXT.DAT will be copied from drive B to the current drive (A) with the same filename.

In the second example, all files on drive A that have a filename extension of .DAT will be copied to the diskette in drive B with no changes in either the primary filename or the filename extension.

In the third example, PROGRAM.BAS will be copied from the diskette in drive A to the diskette in drive B with the filename, PROGRAM.BAK.

The final example illustrates the use of a device name with the COPY command. Here, TEXT.DAT on drive A is copied to the console device.

DATE

Type: External

The DATE command is used to enter or change the system date. This date is recorded in the directory entry for any files which are either created or modified.

Configuration

DATE

When the DATE command is executed, the following prompt will appear.

```
Current date is mm-dd-yy
Enter new date: __
```

mm--must be 1 or 2 integers from 1-12.
dd--must be 1 or 2 integers from 1-31.
yy--must be 2 digits from 80-99.

An invalid entry will result in the following message:

Invalid date

If the date displayed is correct, you can leave it unchanged by just pressing Enter.

Either the hyphen (-) or the slash (/) can be used as delimiters when entering the date.

DIR

Type: Internal

The DIR or Directory command can be used to list the directory entries for all the files on a diskette or to determine whether a specific file is on the diskette.

Configuration

DIR [*d:*] [*filename* [*.ext*]]

The directory display includes the filename, the file's size in bytes, and the date the file list was updated.

Examples

A > DIR
A > DIR A:PROGRAM.BAS

The first example would display a directory listing for the diskette in drive A. The second example would display a directory listing for a file named, PROGRAM.BAS, if that file is found on the diskette in drive A.

DISKCOMP

Type: External

The DISKCOMP or Compare Diskette command is used to compare the contents of the diskette in the first drive with the contents of the diskette in the second drive. Note that the Compare Diskette command is used to compare entire diskettes, while the COMP command is used to compare two files. DISKCOMP is generally used following a DISKCOPY operation.

Configuration

DISKCOMP [*d*:] [*d*:]

You might note that the drive specifiers are optional. If both parameters are omitted, a single drive compare operation will be performed on the default drive. If the first drive specifier is included but the second omitted, the current drive will be used as the second parameter.

You will be prompted by DISKCOMP to insert the diskettes in the proper drives at the appropriate times. DISKCOMP will compare each of the 40 tracks. The track numbers (0-39) will be displayed with a message when they are found not to be equal.

After the comparison has been completed, DISKCOMP will display the following prompt:

Compare more diskettes? (Y/N)

Enter Y if you wish to make more comparisons. Enter N if you wish to end DISKCOMP.

DISKCOPY

Type: External

Configuration

DISKCOPY [*d*:] [*d*:]

If both drive specifiers are omitted, a single drive copy operation will be performed on the default drive. If the second drive specifier is omitted, the current drive will be used as the target drive.

You will be prompted by DISKCOPY to enter the diskettes at the proper time. When DISKCOPY has finished copying, the following message will be displayed:

Copy another? (Y/N)

If N is entered, DISKCOPY will be ended. If Y is entered, another copy operation will be performed after the user enters the data required by the prompts.

If a diskette has had a large amount of file creation and deletion activity, the disk space may be allocated unevenly. A diskette with uneven space allocation can result in less than optimum diskette performance because the disk read/write head must move further to find, read, and write files.

If a diskette contains uneven space allocation, it is recommended that you use the Copy command rather than DISKCOPY. COPY writes files sequentially i.e. the first free sector found is allocated for the next file. Therefore, COPY eliminates the uneven space problem.

ERASE

Type: Internal

The ERASE command is used to erase the file specified.

Configuration

ERASE *filespec*

The filename match character can be used in the filename. The system files IBMBIO.COM, IBMDOS.COM, and BADTRACK may not be erased.

FORMAT

Type: External

The FORMAT command is used to initialize the diskette in the drive specified. FORMAT also will check the diskette for any defective tracks and prepare the diskette to accept DOS files by initializing the directory, file allocation table, and system loader. All blank diskettes must be formatted before they can be used by DOS.

Configuration

FORMAT [*d*:][/*S*]

If the optional /S is specified in the FORMAT command, the following DOS operating system files will also be copied from the current drive to the diskette.

IBMBIO.COM
IBMDOS.COM
COMMAND.COM

Whenever a diskette is formatted, any existing data will be erased.

If any defective tracks are discovered during the formatting of a diskette, these tracks are assigned to a file called BADTRACK. This prevents the defective tracks from being used by a data file.

The CHKDSK command can be used to determine whether or not any defective tracks were discovered. If /S was not included in the FORMAT command, then CHKDSK should report zero disk files. If defective tracks were found, they will be included in the BADTRACK file, and CHKDSK will report one file.

If /S was used during the formatting process, CHKDSK will report three files if no defective tracks were discovered (IBMBIO.COM, IBMDOS.COM and COMMAND.COM). If defective tracks were found, CHKDSK will report the presence of four files.

MODE

Type: External

The MODE command is used to set the mode of operation on a printer or on a monitor connected to the Color/Graphics Monitor Adapter.

Configuration 1 (Printer)

MODE LPT#:[,*n*][,*m*]

The preceding configuration is used to set the parameters for the printer. The # should be replaced with a 1, 2, or 3 which specifies the printer number. The *n* should be either 80 or 132, which specifies the number of characters per line. The *m* should be either 6 or 8, which is the number of lines per inch. The default parameters are 80 characters per line and 6 lines per inch.

Configuration 2
(for monitor connected to Color/Graphics Monitor Adapter)

MODE [*n*,][,*m*][,*T*]

The preceding command is used to set the parameters for a monitor connected to the Color/Graphics Monitor Adapter. The *n* can either be 40 or 80, which specifies the number of characters per line. The *m* can either be R or L, which are used to shift the display to the left or right.

The *T* is used to display a test pattern which can be used to help align the display. When *T* is specified, a prompt will ask the user if the screen has been properly aligned. If a Y is entered, the command will end. If N is entered, the screen will shift again in the direction specified by *m*.

PAUSE

Type: Internal

The PAUSE command is used to cause the system to temporarily stop.

Configuration

PAUSE [*remark*]

After PAUSE is executed, the system will display the optional remark as well as the following message:

Strike any key when ready . . .

PAUSE commands often are inserted within batch files at critical points to allow the user to change a diskette or to display a message. By pressing any key, execution of the batch file can be continued.

REM

Type: Internal

The REM or Remark command is used to display remarks within a batch file.

Configuration

REM [*remark*]

The optional remark can consist of a string of up to 123 bytes. The remarks are displayed when the execution within the batch file reaches a Remark Command. If a REM command is used without an optional remark, a blank line will appear.

RENAME

Type: Internal

The RENAME command is used to change a file's name.

Configuration

RENAME *filespec filename* [*.ext*]

The RENAME command will change the name of the file specified in the first parameter to the filename specified in the second parameter. The filename match characters (? and *) can be used in the RENAME parameters.

Examples

```
RENAME B:PROGRAM1 PROGRAM2
RENAME B:PROGRAM2  *.BAS
```

In the first example, PROGRAM1 on drive B is renamed to PROGRAM2. In the second example, PROGRAM2 is renamed as PROGRAM2.BAS.

SYS

Type: External

The SYS command is used to transfer the operating system from the default drive to the drive specified in the command.

Configuration

SYS *d:*

The following files will be copied to the drive specified when SYS is executed:

IBMBIO.COM
IBMDOS.COM

When using SYS, the diskette in the drive specified by the command must previously have been formatted with the FORMAT command and /S option, so as to allocate the specific locations on the diskette for the system files. If this was not done, SYS will not be able to transfer the operating system files, as diskette locations had not previously been allocated for these files.

The SYS command was designed to be used to transfer a copy of the DOS files to an applications program diskette formatted to use DOS, but sold without DOS.

TIME

Type: External

The TIME command allows the user to change the system time.

Configuration

TIME

When TIME is executed, the following message will appear.

```
Current time is hh:mm:ss.xx
Enter new time
```

The following abbreviations are used:

hh - for hours. One or two digits (0-23).
mm - for minutes. One or two digits (0-59).
ss - for seconds. One or two digits (0-59).
xx - for hundredths of seconds. One or two digits (0-99).

Note that colons separate the hours, minutes, and seconds while a period separates seconds and hundredths of seconds.

Example

```
A > TIME
Current Time is 01:22:15.29
Enter New Time: 12:16:12.31
```

TYPE

Type: Internal

The TYPE command is used to display a file's contents on the screen.

Configuration

TYPE *filespec*

If you press Ctrl-Prtsc before execution of the TYPE command, the file's contents will be displayed on the printer as well as the screen.

Example

A ><u>TYPE B:PROGRAM1.BAS</u> ↵

The preceding example will cause the contents of PROGRAM1.BAS located on drive B to be displayed.

Chapter 7. DOS Commands: EDLIN, LINK and DEBUG

Introduction to EDLIN (The Line Editor)

DOS's line editor (EDLIN) can be used to create, modify and display **source** or **text** files. A source file is an assembly language program in source language format which has not been assembled.

The text of the files which are being processed by EDLIN are divided into lines. The length of these lines can vary -- with a maximum of 253 characters per line.

Numbers are automatically assigned to these lines. Although these line numbers are displayed during the editing session, they are not actually present within the file being edited.

Executing EDLIN

EDLIN is executed using the following configuration:

EDLIN *filespec*

If the file specified does exist on the current drive, the file will be loaded into memory until it is 75% filled. If enough memory is available to load the entire file, the following message and prompt will be displayed.

```
End of input file
*_
```

If the entire file cannot be loaded, the file will be loaded line by line until memory has become 75% filled. The EDLIN prompt (*) will then be displayed.

When only a portion of a file has been loaded, only those lines which have been loaded into memory can be edited. Before you can edit the remaining lines, some of the edited lines in memory must be written to the diskette so as to free available memory for the unedited lines.

If the file specified in EDLIN is not present on the designated drive, a new file with that name will be created. When this occurs, the following message and prompt will appear:

```
New file
*_
```

You may not enter lines into this new file after issuing an Insert lines command (discussed later).

When the editing process is ended, both the original and the edited files will be saved on a diskette. The original file will be renamed with the same primary filename and an extension of .BAK. The new file has the filename specified in the EDLIN command.

When EDLIN is executed, if a file exists with the same primary name as the file specified and the filename extension .BAK, that file will be erased. A new file with the same primary name as the file specified and the extension $$$ will be created. This file will eventually be used to hold the edited file, and its filename extension will be changed from $$$ to that specified in the EDLIN command.

A file with an extension of .BAK cannot be edited. If you wish to edit such a file, first use the Rename command to change the filename extension from .BAK.

EDLIN Command Summary

In this section, we will discuss the various commands that can be used with EDLIN.

All EDLIN commands consist of a single letter except the Edit line command. Commands generally are used with parameters. Both commands and parameters can be entered in upper-case, lower-case, or a mixture of both.

Generally, commands and their parameters are separated by delimiters (space or commas) to improve their readability. However, this is not required. Delimiters are only required between two adjacent line numbers.

DOS commands can be aborted by pressing Ctrl-Break. A DOS command will be executed when Enter is pressed at the end of the command. If a large amount of data is being displayed as a result of a DOS command, you can hold the screen by pressing Ctrl-Numlock. To continue the scrolling, press any key.

The following parameters will be used in our discussion of DOS commands.

line	Three entries can be made for *line*. A integer from 1-65529 can be used to identify a particular line.
.	A period (.) can be used to identify the **current line.** The current line is used to mark the location of the last change in the file being edited. This does not have to be the last line displayed. The current line is identified by an asterisk which appears between the line number and the first character in the line.
#	A pound sign (#) is used to identify the line after the final line in memory.
n	This specifies the number of lines to be written to the diskette or read from the diskette. The *n* parameter is used only with the Write Lines and Append Lines commands. These commands are used when the file being edited is too large to fit in memory.
string	One or more characters is to be entered in place of this parameter. These characters represent text to either be searched for, replaced, deleted, or to be used in place of other text. The *string* parameter is only used with the search text and replace text parameters.

Append Lines EDLIN Command

The Append Lines command is used to append lines from the diskette to the file in memory being edited. These lines are added to the end of that file.

Configuration

[*n*] A

The Append lines command is only used when the file being edited was too large to fit in memory.

If no *n* is included, the number of lines to be appended are not specified in the command. In this case, lines will be appended until available memory is 75% filled.

When the last line of a diskette file has been appended into memory, the following message will be displayed:

End of input file

Delete Lines EDLIN Command

The Delete Lines command is used to delete a specified group of lines from the file being edited.

Configuration

[*line*] [,*line*] D

When lines are deleted, the line following the last line deleted will become the current line in memory. The current line and those lines following it will be renumbered.

If both parameters are included, that range of lines will be deleted. If the first parameter is deleted (,*line* D), the deletion will begin with the current line and continue to the line specified by the second parameter. (Note the comma's inclusion to denote the second parameter.)

If the second parameter is omitted (*line* D or *line*, D), only the single line named will be deleted.

If both parameters are omitted, only the current line will be omitted. The following line will become the new current line.

Edit Line EDLIN Command

This command is used to enter the line number of the line to be edited.

Configuration

[*line*]

If no entry is made (the Enter key is pressed), this indicates that the line following the current line is to be edited.

When this command is executed, the line number entered and its contents will be displayed. The line number will then be repeated on the following line.

This line may then be edited using the Control and Editing keys, or the line may be completely replaced by entering new text. When editing is complete, press Enter, and the edited line will be placed in the current file where it will become the current line.

If after reviewing the line displayed by Edit line, you decide not to edit it, you can either press Ctrl-Break, ESC, or the Enter key (if the cursor is at the first position) to abort the command.

End Edit EDLIN Command

The End Edit command is used to end EDLIN and to save the file being edited on diskette.

Configuration

E

The file being edited will be stored on a diskette with the name specified when the EDLIN command was issued. The original version of the newly edited file will be saved with the filename extension .BAK.

When editing files, be certain there is enough available diskette space to store both the original file and its back-up. If enough space is not available, that part of the file in memory for which diskette space is not available will be lost.

When the EDLIN command has been ended, the DOS prompt will appear.

Insert Lines EDLIN Command

The Insert Lines command is used to insert lines of text in front of the line number specified. If no line number is specified, the insertion will occur before the current line.

Configuration

[*line*] I

If the specified line number is greater than the highest existing line number or is specified as #, the insertion will be made after the final line in memory.

As each new line is typed in, press the Enter key. A new line number will be displayed every time Enter is pressed. To end the Insert command, press the Ctrl-Break keys.

The line following the inserted lines will become the current line. Both the current line and all following lines will be renumbered to reflect the insertion.

List Lines EDLIN Command

The List Lines command is used to display the lines specified in the command. The current line is not changed by this command.

Configuration

[*line*][,*line*] L

If the first parameter is omitted, the display will begin 11 lines before the current line, and 23 lines in total will be displayed.

If the second parameter is omitted, a total of 23 lines will be displayed beginning with the specified line.

If both parameters are omitted, a total of 23 lines will be displayed. These include the 11 lines immediately preceding the current line, and the 11 lines immediately following the current line. If there are not 11 lines preceding the current line, additional lines following the current line will be displayed to total 23 lines.

Quit Edit EDLIN Command

The Quit Edit command is used to end the editing session without any of the editing changes being saved.

Configuration

Q

When the Q command is used, the following prompt will appear.

Abort edit (Y/N)?

If you wish to exit EDLIN with no changes made in the original file, enter Y. Otherwise, enter N and continue editing.

Note that when you execute EDLIN, your previous back-up copy (with the .BAK filename extension) will have been erased. Therefore, exercise caution when using the Q command as your back-up file will have been erased.

Replace Text EDLINE Command

The Replace Text command is used to replace existing string data with new data.

Configuration

[*line*] [,*line*] [?] R*string* [F6*string*]

The Replace Text command will replace the characters specified in the first string with those specified in the second string in the range of lines given preceding the R. If a second string is not specified, the characters given in the first string will be deleted. The last line changed will be the current line.

The optional parameter ? is used to display a prompt (OK?) after each line to be modified. If a Y or Enter is pressed, the modification will be made. Otherwise, the modification will not be made.

If the first *line* parameter is omitted, the default value will be line one. If the second *line* parameter is omitted, the second line value will default to the last line. If both *line* parameters are omitted, all lines in memory will be searched.

Note that the F6 key is used to separate the two strings. A Ctrl-Z entry can also be used to separate these.

Search Text EDLIN Command

The Search Text command is used to search a specified range of lines for a designated string.

Configuration

[*line*] [,*line*] [?] *Sstring*

Unless the ? parameter is used, the first line to contain a matching string will be displayed and the search will end. This line will become the current line.

If no match is found, the following message will be displayed:

Not found

and the search will end. The current line will remain the same.

If the optional ? parameter is included, the following prompt will be displayed when a match is encountered.

OK?

If Y or Enter is pressed in response to this prompt, the matching line will become the current line and the Search Text command will end.

If any other entry is made, the search will continue until another match is found or until all the lines in the specified range have been searched.

If the first *line* parameter is omitted, the default value is the first line. If the second *line* parameter is omitted, the default value is the last line. If both are omitted, all lines in memory will be searched.

Write Lines EDLIN Command

The Write lines command is used to write to the diskette file from the lines being edited in memory. The lines are written beginning with the first line.

Configuration

[*n*] W

The Write lines command need only be used in instances where the file being edited was too large to fit into memory. In these cases, edited lines in memory must be written to the diskette file before additional lines can be appended with the Append Lines command.

LINK (or Linker)

LINK is a program that will perform the following:

1. Combine object modules.
2. Search library files for definitions of unresolved external references.
3. Resolve external cross-references.
4. Produce a listing of the resolution of external references and error messages.
5. Produce a relocatable load module.

The Linker is used with the following types of files:

Input Files

- Object files produced by the assembler with filename extensions of .REL and override features.

- Object files produced by the compiler with filename extensions of .OBJ and override features.

- Library files produced by the compiler.

- Automatic Response files produced by the user.

Output Files

- Listing Files used by the user with a filename extension of .MAP and overrride features.

- Run Files used by the COMMAND.COM relocatable loader with a filename extension of .EXE and no override features.

Segment, Group and Class

Three terms are used in conjunction with LINK; segment, group, and class. An understanding of these terms will assist you in understanding LINK.

A **segment** is a consecutive area of memory which can be up to 64K bytes long. A segment may be located at any address in memory as long as it is on a paragraph boundary (16-byte).

The four segment registers are used to define a segment. Every 16 bit address is an offset from the segment's starting point. The contents of a segment are addressed via a segment/register offset pair.

The contents of the different parts of the segment are set during machine language generation. However, the size and location of a segment are not determined during machine language generation, because this may be changed when different segments are combined by the Linker.

The final location of a program in memory is determined when it is loaded.

A **group** is a set of segments which will fit within a 64K byte segment of memory. The assembler or compiler determines which segments are to be included in a group.

Groups are used for addressing segments in memory. The different parts of segments within the group are addressed via a segment base pointer plus an offset.

A **class** is a collection of segments. The segments are ordered within a class in the same order that they are found in the object files by LINK. For one class to be placed before another in memory, one segment in the first class must precede all segments in the seond class in the order input by LINK. The class name is given by the assembler or the compiler.

VM.TMP

The Linker program makes use of as much available memory as is possible when it creates the load module. If the load module will not fit in the available memory, a temporary file named VM.TMP will be created on the diskette in the current drive to hold the overflow.

A message will be displayed when a VM.TMP file is created. Once a VM.TMP file has been created, the diskette containing that file should be left in place until the Linker program is ended. When LINK ends, the VM.TMP file will be deleted.

LINK Prompts

After the LINK program has been executed, a series of nine prompts will be displayed. These prompts may be answered one by one via the keyboard or all at once via a special diskette file.

LINK will prompt for the names of the object, run, list, and library files as well as for any optional parameters that might control the linking. When the linking has been accomplished, control will return to DOS.

The various LINK prompts and their responses are listed below.

- Prompt - OBJECT MODULES:
  Response - *filespec*
  Default value - none

- Prompt - RUN FILE:
  Response - *filespec*
  Default value - none

- Prompt - LIST FILE:
  Response - *filespec*
  Default value - run file primary name + .MAP

- Prompt - LIBRARIES:
  Response - *filespec . . .*
  Default - no library search

- Prompt - PUBLICS:
  Response - *Y or N;* Y gives all global symbols with definitions
  Default value - N

- Prompt - LINE NUMBERS:
  Response - *Y or N;* Y includes line numbers in the LIST file.
  Default value - N

- Prompt - STACK SIZE
  Response - A non-zero decimal entry sets the stack size in the RUN file.
  Default value - original stack size (0)

- Prompt - LOAD LOW
  Response - *Y or N;* Y results in the RUN file being loaded in low memory upon execution.
  Default value - N

- Prompt - DISALLOCATION:
  Response - *Y or N;* Y results in data being loaded at high end of data segment.
  Default value - N

Each of the LINK prompts will be discussed in detail in the following sections.

Object (Input) Modules

The file specifications for the files to be linked should be entered. If the filename extension is not included in the file specification, a filename extention of .OBJ or .REL will be assumed. If an object module has a filename extension other than .OBJ or .REL, the filename extension must be included in the filename specification.

If more than one filename specification is entered under object modules, these multiple entries must be separated by either commas or spaces.

If an object module that was specified cannot be found, a prompt will be displayed that instructs the user to insert the diskette containing the object module specified. Therefore, files from several different diskettes can be included.

If you are using a system with just one disk drive, you can use this diskette changing procedure if the VM.TMP file has not been opened. If VM.TMP has been opened, a prompt message to that effect will be displayed.

If you are using a system with more than one disk drive, you must be careful to avoid the diskette in the default drive if that diskette contains VM.TMP. If a diskette must be exchanged, the second drive should be used.

Run (Executable) File

The file specification entered will be used to hold the Run file that was created as a result of LINK. All Run files are automatically assigned a filename extension of .EXE.

The /P option can be used following the entry of a file specification to display a message to the operator. This message will prompt the operator to insert the diskette that is to receive the Run file. If the /P option is used, the Run file should be specified to be placed on the second drive.

List File

Usually, the List file will be placed on the diskette that is to receive the Run file. The List file will include an entry for each of the segments in the various object modules as well as the offset in the Run file. If a file specification is not entered for the List file, the same primary name as is used for the Run file will be assigned along with a filename extension of .MAP.

Libraries

If the Enter key is pressed without any entries, a library search will not be undertaken. If one or more file specifications are entered, LINK will search the library files for the file specified.

If found, that library file will be processed as another object file. If the library file referenced is not found, a prompt will be displayed that asks that the identifier of the drive containing the library file be entered.

Between 1 and 8 library file specifications can be entered. When more than one file specification is entered, each must be separated with a comma or blank space.

Publics

If a Y is entered, LINK will list all public or global symbols previously defined in the input modules. LINK will list the value and segment offset location in the Run file of each symbol. The symbols will be listed at the end of the List file.

Line Numbers

A response of Y will instruct LINK to include the line numbers and addresses of the source statements in the input modules in the List file.

Stack Size

The operator may either enter any integer up to 65536 or may just press the Enter key.

Any entry from 1 to 511 will default to 512. An entry of zero will default to pressing Entry with no other data entered.

If zero was entered or if Enter was pressed, the original stack size provided by the assembler or compiler will be used.

An integer value entry will represent the stack size in bytes. If the size of the stack is too small, when the load module is executed, the results may be unexpected.

At least one of the input modules must have a stack allocation specified. If a stack allocation statement was not specified, the following message will be displayed:

WARNING: NO STACK STATEMENT

Load Low:

If a Y is entered, the Run file will be placed as low in memory as possible. A response of N will cause the loader to place the Run file as high in memory as possible. If you are using PASCAL, a response of Y will be required.

Disallocation

If a response of N is given, LINK will load all data which is defined to exist in a group known as DGROUP at the low end of the data segment, beginning with an offset of zero.

If a response of Y is given, LINK will load all data in DGROUP at the high end of the data segment. At run time, the data space pointer will begin at the lowest possible address that continues to allow addressability to all data elements in the group.

If the previous Load Low response had been N (which loaded the module high), an entry of Y will allow any free memory below DGROUP to be allocated by the application and still be addressable by the same data pointer.

If the response to Disallocation was N, the only memory that can be addressed by the data space pointer will be that included in DGROUP.

Link Special Characters

LINK uses two special characters in entering responses to the command prompts, the ampersand (&) and the exclamation point (!).

An ampersand can be used to extend the current line in situations where a number of lengthy entries are required. By entering an ampersand at the end of a line, it will be extended and responses can continue to be entered. When Enter is pressed, the entry will have been completed.

An exclamation point followed by pressing Enter can be used to select the defaults for the various prompts. Of course, this is only available after the object module and Run file prompts have been responded to.

Executing LINK

LINK can be executed in either of two ways. You can execute LINK from your keyboard by typing in the following:

LINK

LINK will then be loaded into memory, and the nine prompts will appear, one by one. If an incorrect response is made to one of the prompts, the user can press Ctrl-Break to exit LINK.

The second method of executing LINK involves the use of an Automatic Response File. The Automatic Response File will contain the responses to the various LINK prompts. The responses must be in the same order as the LINK prompts appear. The Automatic Response File must be created before LINK can be executed in this fashion.

To execute LINK with an automatic response file, enter the following:

LINK *filespec*

where *filespec* is the file specification of the Automatic Response File.

The greater than and less than signs (< >) may be used within Automatic Response Files to prompt for operator entries. This is shown in the Automatic Response File example below:

```
FILE1, FILE2, FILE3&
<ENTER ADDITONAL MODULES >
NEWFILE
LISTFILE
DATA2.LIB
Y
Y
O
N
N
```

When execution of LINK reaches the line, <ENTER ADDITIONAL MODULES>, that line will appear on the video display. The user can then enter any additional object modules followed by Enter, or can just press Enter. After this entry has been completed, LINK execution will continue.

Notice the use of the ampersand at the end of the first line in the sample Automatic Response File. This will cause any responses to the user prompt to be included with the other object modules.

Introduction To DEBUG

The DEBUG program has several uses. First of all, DEBUG can be used to execute **object files,** which can be defined as executable programs in machine language notation. DEBUG can also be used to display, modify, or alter any file. DEBUG also allows the user to test his programs, correct any problems in it, and then execute it. This allows the user to immediately determine whether or not his changes to the program worked.

Executing DEBUG

DEBUG can be executed by using the following configuration.

DEBUG [*filespec*]

If a file specification is entered, the DEBUG program will load the file specified into memory. The user can then enter various commands that will display, modify, or execute that file.

If a file specification is not entered, the user must load the desired file into memory with the Name and Load commands, or else work with the existing memory contents.

When DEBUG begins, the registers and flags are set to the following values for the program file in question.

> The Instruction Pointer (IP) is set to 0100H. (H = hexadecimal).
>
> The Stack Pointer (SP) is set to the lower of either the end of the segment or the low point of the transient position of COMMAND.COM. At offset 6, the segment size will be lessened by

100H to allow for a stack of that dimension.

The segment registers (CS, DS, ES, and SS) are set to the low end of free memory. This is the first segment after the end of the DEBUG program.

The rest of the registers (AX, BX, CX, DX, BP, SI, and DI) are all initialized to a value of zero if DEBUG is executed without a file specification. If DEBUG is executed with a file specification, the CX register will hold the specified file's length in bytes.

All flags are initialized to their clear values.

The default disk transfer address is set to 80H.

DEBUG Command Parameters

In the remainder of this chapter, we will discuss the various DEBUG commands. The following parameters will be used in our discussion.

address — Data can be entered for this parameter using any of the following.

- The entry can consist of an alphabetic segment register followed by an offset value (ex. CS:0200).
- The entry can also consist of a segment address followed by an offset value (ex. 1EF:0100).
- The entry can consist of an offset value by itself (ex. 0200), in which case the command will use a default segment.

byte — The entry for this parameter can either be a one or two character hexadecimal value.

drive — The drive from which data is to be loaded or to which data is to be written should be entered. An entry of zero specifies drive A and an entry of 1 specifies drive B.

filespec The file specification can consist of a drive designator, filename, filename extension, or any one or two of these.

list For this parameter, enter one or more than one *byte* and/or *string* values (discussed later).
For example, the following:

E3 'ABC' 5D "xyx"

has 4 items in the list of which two are byte entries and two are string entries.

port address For this parameter, a 1 to 4 character hexadecimal value should be entered that identifies an 8 or 16 bit port address.

range Either of the following two formats can be entered to indicate the low point and high point of a range.

address address

Ex. CS:200, 100

Note that the second address must be an offset value and that the addresses must be delimited by either a comma or a space.

address L *value*

The *value* refers to the number of bytes (in hexadecimal format) to be processed by the command.

Ex. CS:200 L 12

startsec #sec This entry should consist of 1 to 3 hexadecimal values which give the starting relative sector number and the number of sectors to be loaded or written.

Relative sectors are given numbers sequentially from 0 to 13F beginning at track 0 sector 1.

A maximum of 80H sectors can either be loaded or written with a single command.

string — This entry should consist of characters enclosed in either quote (') or double quote marks.

value — A hexadecimal value of 1 to 4 characters should be entered for this parameter. This entry should specify one of the following:

- The number of bytes that a command should work with.
- The numbers to be added or to be subtracted (Hexarithmetic command).
- The number of instructions to be executed (Trace command).

DEBUG Command Entry

The following general rules apply to the entry of DEBUG commands.

The command is not active until the Enter key has been pressed.

The command entry can be ended by pressing Ctrl-Break.

The various DOS editing and function keys can be used while entering DEBUG commands.

Scrolling of the video display can be halted by pressing Ctrl-Numlock. Press any key for restart.

DEBUG command parameters can be entered in upper case letters, lower case letters, or both.

Commands and their parameters generally are delimited by either a comma or a space to make them more readable. However, delimiters are only required between two successive hexadecimal entries.

When a syntax error is encountered, the line containing the error will be displayed with a pointer denoting the location of the error.

The DEBUG prompt is the hyphen (-).

Dump DEBUG Command

The Dump command is used in DEBUG to send the contents of a portion of memory to the display.

Configuration

D [*address*]
or
D [*range*]

The memory dump is displayed in both hexadecimal and ASC II format. In the hexadecimal format, each byte is displayed in hexadecimal notation. In ASC II format, each byte is displayed as an ASC II character. Any bytes denoted by non-printable ASC II characters will be displayed as a period (.).

When Dump is used with an 80 column video display, 16 bytes will be displayed on each line. A hyphen will separate the 8th and 9th bytes. The line will begin on a 16 byte boundary.

When Dump is used with a 40 column display, 8 bytes will be displayed on each line. Each line will begin on an 8 byte boundary.

When the following configuration is used for Dump:

D [*address*]

the contents of memory will be dumped beginning with the address given.

If D is specified without a parameter, the Dump command will use the *address* directly following the last *address* used by a Dump command. This makes it possible to dump continuous 40 or 80 byte blocks by entering consecutive D commands without parameters.

If D was executed without a parameter and no preceding D command had been given, the *address* used will offset 0100H into the segment that was initialized in the segment registers by DEBUG.

If the Dump command was executed with the following format:

D *range*

the contents of memory in the range specified will be displayed.

Enter DEBUG Command

The Enter Command can be used for two different purposes using the following configuration.

Configuration

E *address* [*list*]

First of all, the Enter command can be used to replace the contents of memory beginning at the location specified in *address* with the values given in *list*.

The Enter command can also be used to sequentially display bytes from memory beginning at the indicated address and make them available for alteration. The following configuration is used for this application of Enter.

E *address*

Once the address and the byte stored at that address are displayed, the following actions can be taken.

> Enter a 1 or 2 character hexadecimal value to replace that addresses existing contents. Press the space bar to advance to the next address.

Then, any of the following steps can be taken.

> Press the space bar to display the next address.
>
> Enter a hyphen to go backwards in memory to display the previous address. You can then change the contents of this address if you so desire.
>
> The Enter command can be ended by pressing the Enter key. The DEBUG prompt (-) will then appear.

Fill DEBUG Command

The Fill command is used to fill the memory addresses specified in *range* with the values given in *list*.

Configuration

F *range list*

If the number of bytes given in *list* is less than the number of bytes included in *range*, the list will be used repeatedly until all of the addresses given in *range* have been filled.

If more values were specified in *list* than were allowed for in the *range*, any extra values in *list* will not be used.

Go DEBUG Command

The Go command is used to execute the program currently being debugged. The Go command includes a feature where the program execution can be stopped when an instruction at a specified address is reached (known as a **breakpoint**). After execution is stopped, the registers, flags, and the next instruction will be displayed.

Configuration

G [= *address*] [*breakpoint address . . .*]

If no = *address* is specified with the command, program execution will start with the current instruction. If = *address* is specified, execution will begin with that address.

If no *breakpoint address* is specified, the program being debugged will be executed. If one or more *breakpoint addresses* are specified, breakpoints will be set at the addresses given. Up to ten breakpoints can be specified.

Hexarithmetic DEBUG Command

The Hexarithmetic command is used to add two hexadecimal values, and also subtract the second value from the first. Both the sum of the two values and the differences will be displayed on the same line in hexadecimal form.

Configuration

H *value value*

Example

H 0A 7
11 03

In the preceding example, the hexadecimal sum of 000A and 0007 is displayed followed by their difference.

Input DEBUG Command

The Input command is used to input and display (in hexadecimal format) one byte from the port specified.

Configuration

I *port address*

Example

I 2D7
5A

In the preceding example, a byte with a hexadecimal value of 5A is read from port 2D7.

Load DEBUG Command

The Load command is used to load a file or diskette sectors into memory.

Configuration

L [*address* [*drive begin sector # sectors*]]

The Load command is used in two different ways. If Load is used with the following configuration:

L *address drive begin sector # sectors*

data will be loaded from the diskette named in *drive*. That data will be loaded into memory beginning at the location specified in *address*. The data will be read from the sector named in *begin sector* until the number of sectors given in *#sectors* has been read.

If the Load command is used without any parameters as shown below:

L

or when Load is used only with the *address* parameter:

L *address*

the file whose file specification is given in the file control block at CS:5C will be loaded. This can be accomplished by giving that file's specification when executing DEBUG or by using the Name command.

If no *address* is given, the file will be loaded beginning at CS:100. If an *address* is specified, the loading will begin at the location specified.

Move DEBUG Command

The Move command can be used to move the contents of memory.

Configuration

M *range address*

The contents of memory in the addresses given by *range* will be moved to the memory locations beginning with and following that specified in *address*.

If the locations specified in *range* and *address* overlap, no data will be lost during the transfer. Where no overlapping occurs, the data in the locations specified in *range* will remain the same.

Name DEBUG Command

The Name command uses the configuration given below:

Configuration

N *filespec* [*filespec. . .*]

The Name command is used for two different purposes. First of all, Name can be used to format file control blocks for the first two file specifications at CS:5C and CS:6C. The file control blocks are used by the Load and Write commands as well as to supply required filenames for the program being debugged.

Secondly, all indicated file specifications as well as any other parameters are placed in a parameter save area at CS:81. The number of characters entered will be placed in CS:80.

If a DEBUG program is begun without a filespec being given, the Name command must be used before a file can be loaded with the L command.

Output DEBUG Command

The Output command is used to send the byte value specified to the output port specified.

Configuration

O *portaddress byte*

Example

O 2D7 2F

The preceding example will send the value 2F to output port 2D7.

Quit Command

The Quit command is used to end the DEBUG program.

Configuration

Q

If the Quit command is used to end DEBUG, the file in memory will not be saved on disk. If you wish that file saved on a disk, you must use the Write command.

Register DEBUG Command

The configuration for the Register command is given below:

Configuration

R [*registername*]

The valid *registernames* are as follows:

AX	BP	SS
BX	SI	CS
CX	DI	IP
DX	DS	PC
SP	ES	F

The Register command can be used for three different purposes. First of all, the Register command can be used to display a single register. The contents of the register chosen will be displayed. The operator will have the option of changing the register's contents.

For example, if the following entry were made:

```
R BX
```

the contents of register BX would be displayed as follows:

```
BX D1F3
: ___
```

At this point, the user can leave the contents of register BX unchanged by just pressing Enter. The contents of register BX can be changed by entering a valid hexadecimal value. When Enter is pressed after the hex value has been entered, the contents of register BX will have been changed to the new value.

The Register command also can be used to display the hexadecimal contents of all of the registers, as well as the alphabetic flag settings, and the next instruction to be executed. This can be effected by the following entry:

```
R
```

Finally, the Register command can be used to display the eight 2-letter alphabetic flag settings (see Table 7-1). The user also has the option of changing these. The flags can be displayed with the following entry:

```
R F
```

Table 7-1. Flag Names and Settings

Flag Name	Set	Clear
Overflow (yes/no)	OV	NV
Direction (decrement/increment)	DN	UP
Interrupt (enable/disable)	EI	DI
Sign (negative/positive)	NG	PL
Zero (yes/no)	ZR	NZ
Auxiliary carry (yes/no)	AC	NA
Parity (even/odd)	PE	PO
Carry (yes/no)	CY	NC

When the preceding command has been entered, the following will be displayed (assuming all flags are set):

OV DN EI NG ZR AC PE CY -___

When the flags have been displayed, the user may then either press Enter to leave the settings unchanged, or he may change any of the flags desired.

A flag is changed by entering its opposite settings code. For example, if the user was working with the preceding display, and he wished to change the first and last flag settings, he could do so with the following entry:

OV DN EI NG ZR AC PE CY -NCNV

Notice that the opposite codes can be entered in any order.

The new flag codes can then be displayed with the following entry:

R F

The following will be displayed:

NV DN EI NG ZR AC PE NC -___

A flag can only be changed once during a Register operation.

Search DEBUG Command

The Search command will search a specified range of addresses for a certain group of characters.

configuration

S *range list*

The Search command will search the addresses given in *range* for the characters specified in *list*.

If a match is found, the address where the match occurs is displayed. If the DEBUG prompt (-) is displayed without any addresses being displayed, no match was found.

Trace DEBUG Command

The Trace command is used with the following configuration.

Configuration

T [= *address*] [*value*]

When used without parameters, the Trace command will execute one or more instructions beginning with the instruction at CS:IP. If an *address* is given, execution will begin at the location specified.

The Trace command assumes that one instruction is to be executed. However, if the *value* parameter is included, that number of instructions will be executed.

The Trace command displays the contents of all registers and flags after each instruction has been executed. The display format used is the same as that used in the Register command.

Unassemble DEBUG Command

The Unassemble command is used to unassemble the instructions specified and to display their addresses and hexadecimal values along with statements resembling assembler statements.

Configuration

U [*address*]
or
U [*range*]

If the Unassemble command is given without a parameter, as shown below:

U

the starting address used by Unassemble will be the next location following the last instruction that was assembled by an Unassemble command. This makes it possible for the user to unassemble continous blocks, by merely entering U.

If the Unassemble command is executed without any parameters, and no Unassemble command had been previously executed, the location used will be an offset of 0100H into the segment originally initialized in the segment registers by the DEBUG program.

The Unassemble command causes 16 bytes to be unassembled at a time if a 40 column display is being used. If an 80 column display is being used, 32 bytes will be unassembled.

If an *address* parameter is specified with the Unassemble command, instructions will be unassembled beginning at that location.

If the Unassembled command is used with the *range* parameter, the instructions within the range specified will be unassembled.

Write DEBUG Command

The Write command is used to write the data being debugged to a diskette.

Configuration

W [*address* [*drive sector sector*]]

When the W command is used with the *address, drive,* and *sector* parameters as per the following configuration:

W *address drive sector sector#*

The data starting at the *address* specified will be written to the diskette contained in the *drive* specified. The data will be written to that diskette beginning with the first *sector* until the number of sectors specified in *sector#* is filled.

When the Write command is used without a parameter or only with the *address* parameter, the Write command will write the file whose file specification is contained in the file control block at CS:5C to the diskette. This is the file which was specified when DEBUG was loaded or when the Name command was executed.

When using the Write command in this manner, you must be certain that the CX register has been set to the number of bytes to be written. Generally, this register is set to the correct value by DEBUG or by the Load command. However, this register may have been changed by either a Go or a Trace command. Before executing the Write command with no parameters or only the *address* parameter, be certain that register CX is holding the correct value.

When the Write command is executed with no parameters, the file beginning at CS:100 will be written to the diskette in the drive specified in the file specification. If the Write command was executed with an *address* parameter, the file beginning at the memory location given in *address* will be written to the diskette in the drive specified.

The debugged file will be written over the file first loaded into memory. If the filename given in the File Control Block did not previously exist, the debugged file will be written into a new file.

Chapter 8. Using IBM BASIC

Introduction

In this chapter, we will discuss the steps involved in using IBM BASIC. We will discuss the three different versions of IBM.BASIC; Cassette, Disk, and Advanced. We will discuss how to start BASIC, how to run a BASIC program, how to enter a BASIC program, as well as some of the concepts of programming in BASIC.

IBM BASIC Versions

The IBM PC uses three different versions of BASIC; Cassette BASIC, Disk BASIC, and Advanced BASIC. Cassette BASIC is contained in 32K of ROM within your PC, while Disk and Advanced BASIC are included on the DOS diskette.

Cassette BASIC assumes that a cassette tape recorder is being used to store program and data files. Cassette BASIC cannot be used with diskettes.

Cassette BASIC forms the heart of the other versions of BASIC, Disk and Advanced. These versions add features not found on Cassette BASIC.

Disk BASIC is included on the IBM DOS system diskette as a separate program. Disk BASIC must be loaded into memory before it can be used. Disk BASIC requires a hardware environment with at least a disk drive and at least 32K of RAM.

Disk BASIC offers other features besides input/output to diskettes that Cassette BASIC does not offer. These include an internal clock which will keep track of the time and date, communications support, and also support for two extra printers.

Advanced BASIC has all of the capabilities of Cassette and Disk BASIC. Advanced BASIC also includes several commands such as PAINT, CIRCLE, and DRAW that allow the user to use advanced graphics if his PC is equipped with the Color/Graphics Monitor Adapter. Advanced BASIC also includes the PLAY statement which can be used to allow your IBM to play melodies.

Advanced BASIC requires a hardware environment with at least one disk drive and at least 48K of RAM. Advanced BASIC like Disk BASIC must be loaded from diskette.

Advanced BASIC includes a feature known as **event trapping**. Event trapping means when a specified event occurs (such as a function key being pressed), the program will respond to that event by branching directly to a specific program line.

BASIC Start-Up Procedure

If your PC has disk drives and you wish to start Cassette BASIC, first be certain that no diskette is inserted in drive A and that the drive door is closed. Next, turn on your computer, and the start-up display for Cassette BASIC will appear.

If your PC is powered on and you wish to start Cassette BASIC, again first be certain that there is no diskette in the A drive and that the drive door is shut. Then, press the Ctrl and Alt keys together. While holding them, press the Del key.

The start-up display for Cassette BASIC will then appear on your screen. The display should include the phrase "Version C" followed by a version number along with the number of free bytes.

To start Disk BASIC, you must first be certain that DOS has been loaded. If this has occurred, then the DOS prompt (A >) will be displayed. To load BASIC, enter the following after the DOS prompt:

A > BASIC

The start-up display for Disk BASIC will then appear on your screen. This will include the phrase Version D followed by a version number along with the number of free bytes.

To start Advanced BASIC, again, you must be sure that DOS has been loaded. The following should be entered after the DOS prompt:

A > BASICA

The start-up display for Advanced BASIC will then appear on the screen. This will include the phrase Version A followed by a version number along with the number of free bytes.

When you are loading Disk or Advanced BASIC, additional parameters can be included with the BASIC or BASICA entry. These parameters can be used for the following purposes:

Set aside storage areas for programs and data.

Set aside storage area for buffers.

Instruct BASIC to load and run a program.

The configuration for the BASIC command with all of its optional parameters is as follows:

BASIC [A] [*filespec*] [/F:*files*] [/S:*bufsize*] [/C:*bufcom*] [/M:*work area*]

The optional parameter *filespec* indicates the file specification of a program that is to be automatically loaded and executed by BASIC. If no filename extension is specified, the extension .BAS will be supplied.

The optional parameter /F:*files* indicates the maximum number of files that are allowed to be open at one time while a BASIC program is being executed. The maximum number allowed is 15. If this parameter is omitted, the number of files open will default to 3.

The optional parameter /S:*bufsize* assigns the buffer size to be used with random files. The default value for the buffer size is 128. The maximum size that may be used is 32767. For maximum performance, IBM recommends that you use a buffer size of 512 bytes for random file buffer size. Note that the record length parameter used with the OPEN statement may not be greater than the number of bytes specified in /S:*bufsize*.

The optional parameter /C:*bufcom* is used to initialize the area to be reserved for the communications receive buffer. This parameter is not used unless the Asynchronous

Communications Adapter is installed on your system. The default value for this parameter is 256 bytes for the receive buffer and 128 bytes for the transmit buffer. IBM recommends that the value /C:1024 be used for high speed lines. If a value of /C:0 is specified, no buffer space will be reserved for communications. In this case, communications support will be disabled when BASIC is loaded.

The optional parameter /M:*work area* can be used to initialize the maximum amount of memory in bytes that can be used as a work area under BASIC. The maximum value that can be used is 64K. The default value is 64K. This parameter is often used to reserve a work area for machine language subroutines.

When specifying these optional parameters (*files, bufsize, bufcom,* and *work area*), a decimal, octal or hexadecimal number must be used. Octal number entries must be preceded by &O and hexadecimal number entries must be preceded by &H.

COMMAND AND EXECUTE MODE

Programming can be accomplished in either of two modes with the IBM Personal Computer, command or execute. The **command** mode is active when the prompt, OK, is displayed on the screen. In the command mode, program lines entered by the user are not immediately executed. These are stored in RAM until the user specifies what the final disposition of the program is to be.

Program statements entered in the command mode must be assigned unique **line numbers.** These line numbers are used by the program to identify the program statements.

The **execute mode** is active when the RUN command is executed. The execute mode can be used to run programs entered under the command mode. Once the program has been run, the computer reverts to the execute mode, and the Ok prompt is displayed. This is shown in the following.

```
OK
100 PRINT 12
200 END
RUN
  12
OK
```

Alt Key and BASIC

The Alt key has a special use in BASIC, in that it allows the user to enter entire BASIC keywords with only one keystroke. The BASIC keywords listed in Table 8-1 will be typed when the associated alphabetic key is pressed while the Alt key is being held down.

Table 8-1. Alt/Alpha BASIC Keyword Abbreviations

BASIC Keyword	Alt + Alpha Key Combination
AUTO	ALT + A
BSAVE	ALT + B
COLOR	ALT + C
DELETE	ALT + D
ELSE	ALT + E
FOR	ALT + F
GOTO	ALT + G
HEX$	ALT + H
INPUT	ALT + I
KEY	ALT + K
LOCATE	ALT + L
MOTOR	ALT + M
NEXT	ALT + N
OPEN	ALT + O
PRINT	ALT + P
RUN	ALT + R
SCREEN	ALT + S

THEN	ALT + T
USING	ALT + U
VAL	ALT + V
WIDTH	ALT + W
XOR	ALT + X

The Alt key can also be used to enter valid ASC II characters not found on the keyboard. This is accomplished by holding the Alt key while entering the three digit ASC II code for the desired character on the numeric key pad.

Entering a BASIC Program

BASIC programs are entered as **program lines.** Any text preceded with a number (**line number**) and ended by pressing the Enter key will be regarded as a program line.

The maximum number of characters that may be included in any one line is 255 including Enter. If a line contains more than 255 characters, those extra characters will be dropped, or **truncated,** when Enter is pressed.

BASIC key words and variable names can be entered in lower case, upper case, or a combination of both. However, these entries will be converted to upper case by the BASIC program editor.

A new line can be added to a BASIC program by merely entering a line number followed by the desired text and Enter. When Enter is pressed, the line will be saved as part of the BASIC program.

A line can be replaced in a BASIC program by entering the same line number followed by the desired text and finally pressing Enter. The new entry will replace the previous line.

To delete a line in an existing program, merely enter the line number of the line to be deleted followed by Enter. A group of lines can be deleted via the DELETE command, and an entire program can be deleted with the NEW Command. These will be discussed in the next chapter.

The methods just described for entering a BASIC program only change the program in memory. To save the program with the changes, the SAVE command must be used. SAVE will be discussed in the next chapter.

BASIC Program Editor

The BASIC Program Editor is what is known as a screen line editor. A screen line editor allows the user to change one line at a time anywhere on the screen. The change is affected when the Enter key is pressed. The keys used in the BASIC Program Editor along with their functions, are listed in Table 8-2.

Table 8-2. BASIC Program Editor Keys

Key	Function
Home	This key can be used to move the cursor to the upper lefthand position on the screen.
Ctrl-Home	This key combination clears the screen and positions the cursor to the "home" position.
↑	Moves cursor up one row (Cursor-Up).
↓	Moves cursor down by one row (Cursor-Down).
←	Moves cursor one position to the left. If the cursor is positioned to the leftmost position, it will 'wrap around' to the right-most position of the preceding line (Cursor Left).

Table 8-2. Basic Program Editor Keys (Cont.)

→	Moves cursor one position to the right. If the cursor is in the rightmost position, it will move to the leftmost position of the next line down (Cursor Right).
Ctrl→	Moves cursor to the next word. Words are groups of characters which begin with either a letter or a number and are separated from other words by blanks or special characters. Ctrl→ is also known as Next Word.
Ctrl←	This key combination is also known as Previous Word. It moves the cursor to the previous word.
End	Moves the cursor to the end of the logical line.
Ctrl-End	Erases from the cursor position to the end of the logical line.
Ins	This sets the insert mode. If the insert mode was off, pressing Ins turns it on. If the insert mode was on, pressing this key turns it off. If the flashing cursor covers the lower half of the character position, the insert mode is on. The insert mode is also turned off when the user presses any of the cursor movement keys or Enter.
Del	This key deletes the character at the current cursor position. All characters to the right of the deleted character are moved one position to the left to fill the space left empty by the deleted character.

Table 8-2. Basic Program Editor Keys (Cont.)

Backspace ←	The Backspace key is identified by ←(like the Cursor Left key). However, the Backspace key is located directly to the left of the Num Lock key. The Backspace key results in the deletion of the last character typed. In other words, the character to the left of the cursor will be erased. The characters to the right of the one deleted will be moved one position to the right to fill the empty position.
ESC	This key will cause the entire line to be erased from the screen when it is pressed anywhere within that line. If the line is a program line, it will not be erased from the program in memory.
Ctrl-Break	This key combination causes the program to return to the direct mode. Any changes made to the line being edited will not be saved.
→|	The Tab key moves the cursor to the next tab stop. Tab stops occur after every eight character positions. When the insert mode is on, pressing the Tab key causes blanks to be inserted from the current cursor position to the next tab stop.

Editing The Current Line

Any of the keys listed in Table 8-2 can be used to edit a line being entered under BASIC. The key combinations used to accomplish most familiar editing functions are listed and described in Table 8-3.

Table 8-3. Editing Key Combinations

Desired Function	Description
Extending Logical Line	A logical line can be extended beyond the boundary of the screen by merely continuing typing. As the end of one video line is reached, the cursor automatically will 'wrap around' to the next screen line. The line feed (Ctrl-Enter) can also be used to extend a logical line to the next video line without typing all the way to the edge of the preceding line. When a line feed is entered, blanks will fill the remaining positions of the current line, and the cursor will move to the next video line. When Enter is pressed, the entire logical line (which may extend over several video lines) will be processed by BASIC.
Changing Characters	Use Cursor Left or other cursor control keys to move the cursor over the incorrect key. Type the correct characters over the incorrect ones.
Erasing Characters	Characters anywhere in the line can be erased with the Del key. Use the cursor control keys to position the cursor over the character to be erased. If the character to be erased was the last one entered, the Backspace key may be used to delete it.

Table 8-3. Editing Key Combinations (Cont.)

Adding Characters	Characters can be added within a line by using the insert mode. After moving the cursor to the position where the new characters are to be entered, press the Ins key to activate the insert mode. Then, type the characters to be added. After the entry has been completed, press Cursor Right or End to turn off the insert mode and to move to the end of the line.
Erasing Only Part of the Line	The remainder of the line beyond the cursor position can be erased by pressing Ctrl-End followed by Enter.
Erasing an Entire Line	While entering a line, the user can erase the entire line by pressing the ESC key. The entire logical line being entered will be erased.

BASIC Reserved Words

Reserved words are words that have a special meaning in BASIC. They include all BASIC commands, statements, function names, and operator names.

Reserved words are not allowed to be used as variable names in BASIC statements. Also, reserved words must be delimited in BASIC statements so that they can be recognized. Generally, words can be delimited through the use of blank spaces or special characters.

Table 8-3 contains a list of the reserved words in IBM BASIC.

Constants

Constants can be defined as values used by BASIC during program execution. Constants may be either of two types; string constants or numeric constants.

A string constant must be enclosed in double quotation marks and can consist of up to 255 characters. The following are examples of string constants.

"ABC DEF"
"2792"
"NY, NY 10017"

Table 8-4. BASIC Reserved Words

ABS	DEFSNG	INSTR
AND	DEFSTR	INT
ASC	DELETE	KEY
ATN	DIM	KILL
AUTO	DRAW	LEFT$
BEEP	EDIT	LEN
BLOAD	ELSE	LET
BSAVE	END	LINE
CALL	EOF	LIST
CDBL	EQV	LLIST
CHAIN	ERASE	LOAD
CHR$	ERL	LOC
CINT	ERR	LOCATE
CIRCLE	ERROR	LOF
CLEAR	EXP	LOG
CLOSE	FIELD	LPOS
CLS	FILES	LPRINT
COLOR	FIX	LSET
COM	FNxxxxxx	MERGE
COMMON	FOR	MID$
CONT	FRE	MKD$
COS	GET	MKI$
CSNG	GOSUB	MKS$
CSRLIN	GOTO	MOD
CVD	HEX$	MOTOR
CVI	IF	NAME
CVS	IMP	NEW
DATA	INKEY$	NEXT
DATE$	INP	NOT
DEF	INPUT	OCT$
DEFDBL	INPUT#	OFF
DEFINT	INPUT$	ON

Table 8-4. BASIC Reserved Words (Cont.)

OPEN	RESTORE	SWAP
OPTION	RESUME	SYSTEM
OR	RETURN	TAB(
OUT	RIGHT$	TAN
PAINT	RND	THEN
PEEK	RSET	TIME$
PEN	RUN	TO
PLAY	SAVE	TROFF
POINT	SCREEN	TRON
POKE	SGN	USING
POS	SIN	USR
PRESET	SOUND	VAL
PRINT	SPACE$	VARPTR
PRINT#	SPC(	WAIT
PSET	SQR	WEND
PUT	STEP	WHILE
RANDOMIZE	STICK	WIDTH
READ	STOP	WRITE
REM	STR$	WRITE#
RENUM	STRIG	XOR
RESET	STRING$	

Numeric constants can either be positive or negative numbers. Commas cannot be used within BASIC numeric constants. Numeric constants in BASIC may be denoted in integer, fixed point, floating point, hex, or octal form.

Integer constants can include any of the whole numbers from -32768 to +32768. Integer constants may not include decimal points.

Fixed point constants include positive or negative real numbers. A real number is one that contains a decimal point.

Floating point constants include positive or negative numbers denoted in scientific notation. A floating point number consists of the mantissa (an integer or fixed point number) followed by the letter E (exponent) or D (double precision) and an optional signed integer (the exponent value).

The E or D can be interpreted as "ten to the power of". For example, the following:

3E2

could be interrupted as 3 times 10 to the power of 2. In fixed point notation, this would evaluate as 300.0 or as 300 in integer form.

Hexadecimal constants can consist of up to four digits preceded with & H. The hexadecimal digits are 0,1,2,3,4,5,6,7,8,9, A, B, C, D, E, and F.

Octal constants can consist of up to six digits preceded by &O or &. The octal digits are 0, 1, 2, 3, 4, 5, 6, and 7.

Integer, Single Precision, and Double Precision

Numeric constants may be stored internally by the computer either as integers, single precision numbers, or double precision numbers.

Constants entered in integer, octal, or hex format are stored in two bytes of memory and are interpreted as integers.

In single precision, up to seven digits can be stored and printed. However, only six digits will be accurate. Single precision constants include any numeric constants which are not integers and which contain seven or fewer digits, which are written in exponential form using E, or which include the trailing decimal point(!).

Examples of single precision numeric constants include:

98.7
12.3!
-1.9E10

With double precision, numbers are stored with up to 17 digits and can be printed up to 16 digits. A double precision constant is any numeric constant that is written with eight or more digits, is written in exponential form with D, or contains a trailing number sign (#).

The following are examples of double precision digits:

297895872
347.0#
-1.93D10

Variables and Variable Names

Variables are names that are used to represent values. There are two different types of variables; numeric and string. Numeric variables must contain a value that evaluates to a number, while a string variable can only contain a string value.

The value assigned to a variable must be consistent with the variable type. Initially, before a value is assigned to a string variable, a string variable is assigned a value of null (or empty) and a numeric variable is assigned a value of zero.

Variable names may consist of letters, numbers, and the decimal point. However, the first character of a variable name must be a letter. In IBM BASIC, variable names may be given any length, however, only the first 40 characters are evaluated by the computer.

A reserved word can be included as a portion of a variable name. However, a reserved word by itself cannot be used as a variable name. For example, DATA.NAME would be a legitimate variable name, as the reserved word, DATA, makes up only a portion of the variable name.

On the other hand, the following would be invalid variable names, as these consist solely of the reserved word DATA.

DATA
DATA$
DATA%

Identifiers are used at the end of variable names to identify the type of data they maybe used with. String variables are ended with the dollar sign, as shown below:

X$ = "JOHN"

Numeric variable names may be used to identify integer, single precision, or double precision values. Numeric variable names may be identified with the following suffixes:

% Integer Variable
! Single Precision Variable
Double Precision Variable

If a suffix is not specified, it will default to a single precision type.

Variable types can also be specified with the following BASIC statements:

DEFINT	DEFSNG
DEFDBL	DEFSTR

These will be discussed in the next chapter.

Array Variables

An **array** is a group of data items which are referred to with a single name. Each of the individual data items included in the array is known as an **element**. Array elements are themselves variables which can be used in BASIC program statements and expressions.

Before an array can be used, the name of the array and the number of its elements must be given. This process is known as dimensioning the array and is accomplished via the DIM statement. The following statement dimensions a single dimension array named A$ consisting of 11 elements.

```
100 DIM A$(10)
```

Each of the elements in the array A$ are variable length strings. These are initialized with a value of null.

Arrays can also be two dimensional in nature. Arrays of more than one dimension are often referred to as **tables**. The following DIM statement will create a table named Z consisting of 4 rows and 5 columns giving a total of 20 elements.

```
110 DIM Z(3,4)
```

Since the variable type was not defined with a suffix, the elements will be assumed to contain single precision values. Initially, the elements will be assigned a value of zero.

The array elements are identified with **subscripts**. A subscript is a number or numbers which identify the position of the element within the array. For example, the elements of array A$ would be assigned the following subscripts.

A$(0)
A$(1)
A$(2)
A$(3)
A$(4)
A$(5)
A$(6)
A$(7)
A$(8)
A$(9)
A$(10)

The first element of array A$ is named A$(0) and the last element is named A$(10). Note that array A$ contains 11 elements even though the subscript of its last element is only 10.

Array Z could be visualized as follows:

columns

rows

Z(0,0)	Z(0,1)	Z(0,2)	Z(0,3)	Z(0,4)
Z(1,0)	Z(1,1)	Z(1,2)	Z(1,3)	Z(1,4)
Z(2,0)	Z(2,1)	Z(2,2)	Z(2,3)	Z(2,4)
Z(3,0)	Z(3,1)	Z(3,2)	Z(3,3)	Z(3,4)

Note that array Z contains 20 elements arranged in 4 rows of 5 columns each. The first element is assigned an address of Z(0,0) and the last is assigned Z(3, 4).

In IBM BASIC, if an array element is used in a program before that array has been dimensioned, the array will be assumed to have been dimensioned with a subscript of 10. For example, if the following statement is encountered:

```
100 F(3) = 100
```

and array F had not been dimensioned, F will be dimensioned as a single dimensioned array consisting of the following 11 elements:

F(0) F(1) F(2) F(3) F(4) F(5) F(6) F(7) F(8) F(9) F(10)

It is recommended that you dimension arrays in your program before using the elements from that array in a statement or expression.

Arithmetic Operators

Arithmetic operators are used to perform mathematical operations on numeric and string constants and variables. The arithmetic operators are listed in Table 8-5 in their order of evaluation.

Most of the arithmetic operators will already be familiar to you. However, two of them, integer division and Modulo arithmetic, may not be familiar.

In integer division, the operand is rounded to an integer value before the division is performed. The quotient is also truncated to an integer. For example, in the following expression:

```
A = 37.98 \ 7.87
```

A would evaluate to 4.

Table 8-5. Arithmetic Operators

Symbol	Operation	Example
∧	Exponentiation	A ∧ B
-	Negation	-A
*	Multiplication	A*B
/	Floating Point Division	A/B
\	Integer Division	A\B
MOD	Modulo Arithmetic	X MOD Y
+	Addition	A + B
-	Subtraction	A-B

Modulo arithmetic gives the integer value that is the remainder of an integer division operation. In the following expression:

A = 10MOD3

A would evaluate to 1.

The order of evaluation of arithmetic operations can be changed with the use of parentheses. The expressions enclosed within parentheses will be evaluated first.

Relational Operators

Relational operators are used to compare two values which may both be either numeric or string. If the relational comparison evaluates as true, a value of –1 is returned. If false, a value of 0 is returned. The relational operators are listed in Table 8-6. Arithmetic operations are always performed before relational operators.

Table 8-6. Relational Operators

Symbol	Operation	Example
=	Equality	A = B
< > or ><	Inequality	A<>B; A><B
<	Less Than	A < B
>	Greater Than	A > B
< = or = <	Less Than or Equal To	A<= B; A =<B
> = or = >	Greater Than or Equal To	A>= B; A =>B

Relational operations using numeric operations are fairly straightforward. However, relational operations using string values may prove confusing to the first-time computer user. Strings are compared by taking the ASC II value for each character in the string one at a time and comparing the codes.

If the strings are of the same length, then the string containing the first character with a lower code number is the lesser. If the length of the strings are unequal, then the shorter string is the lesser. Blank spaces are counted and have an ASC II value of 32.

The following comparisons between strings would all evaluate as true.

“ABC” = “ABC”
“ABC ” > “ABC”
“aAA” > “AAA”
“Alfred” < “Zachary”
A$ < Z$ where A$ = “Alfred” and Z$ = “Zachary”

Note that all string constants must be enclosed in quotation marks when used as constants.

Logical Operators

Logical or Boolean operations take a combination of true/false tests and return a final result of true or false. Logical operations are performed on numeric values.

The logical operators are NOT (logical complement), AND (cojunction), OR (disjunction), XOR (exclusive or), IMP (implication), and EQV (equivalence). Logical operators use truth tables for evaluation purposes. These are given in Illustration 8-1.

Illustration 8-1. Truth Tables

NOT

X	NOT X
T	F
F	T

AND

X	Y	X AND Y
T	T	T
T	F	F
F	T	F
F	F	F

OR

X	Y	X OR Y
T	T	T
T	F	T
F	T	T
F	F	F

Illustration 8-1. Truth Tables (Cont.)

XOR

X	Y	X XOR Y
T	T	F
T	F	T
F	T	T
F	F	F

IMP

X	Y	X IMP Y
T	T	T
T	F	F
F	T	T
F	F	T

EQV

X	Y	X EQV Y
T	T	T
T	F	F
F	T	F
F	F	T

T - indicates a true, or non-zero value.

F - indicates a false, or zero value.

Logical operators often are used to set up decisions and then branch program logic based on the result. Logical operators often are used with relational operators. For example, in the following:

```
100 IF < 0 AND Y > 10 THEN 200
```

if both of the relational operations (X < 10, Y > 10) evaluate as true, then the program logic will branch to line 200.

Logical operations are performed after relational and arithmetic operations.

Files

A **file** is a collection of related data. Files are generally stored on a peripheral device, such as a diskette or magnetic tape. Data can be input from or output to a file. The specific file to which data is to be sent or from which data is to be received must be identified with an OPEN statement before any input/output operations can be undertaken. When a file is identified in an OPEN statement, it is assigned a specific number known as a **file number**. A file number can either be a number, a numeric variable, or an expression that evaluates to a number. After a file has been OPEN'ed, it will be identified via that file number.

In Cassette BASIC, file numbers of 1, 2, 3, or 4 may be assigned. Therefore, a maximum of four files can be open at any one time in Cassette BASIC. In Disk and Advanced BASIC, the file numbers that can be used when BASIC is loaded without the IF: option are 1, 2, and 3. The IF: option allows up to 15 file numbers to be used with Disk or Advanced BASIC.

Filenames

A file is described with a **file specification** or **filespec.** File specifications take the following form:

device:filename

where the device gives the file's location and filename specifies the name of the file. In some instances, both the device and filename need not be included in the file specification. The colon must be included in the file specification in instances where the filename is not included but the device name is. In cases where the device name is not included in the file specification but the filename is, the colon need not be included.

Device names can be made up of from one to four characters followed by the colon. A list of device names is given in Table 8-7.

Certain rules must be followed when assigning filenames. Filenames to be used with the cassette unit must consist of eight or less characters. Filenames to be used with diskettes can be made up of two parts; a primary filename and a filename extension. The primary filename can consist of up to eight characters, while the filename extension can consist of up to three characters. Cassette filenames may not include a filename extension.

Table 8-7. Device Names

Device Name	Interpretation
KYBD:	Keyboard. Used in all versions of BASIC for input.
SCRN:	Screen. Used in all versions of BASIC for output.
LPT1:	First printer. Used in all versions of BASIC for output.
LPT2:	Second printer. Used only in Disk and Advanced versions of BASIC for output.
LPT3:	Third printer. Used only in Disk and Advanced versions of BASIC for output.
COM1:	First asynchronous communications adapter. Used only in Disk and Advanced BASIC for input and output.

Table 8-7. Device Names (Cont.)

COM2:	Second asynchronous communications adapter. Used only in Disk and Advanced BASIC for input and output.
CAS1:	Cassette tape unit. Used in all versions of BASIC for input and output.
A:	First or system disk drive. Used in Disk and Advanced versions of BASIC for input and output.
B:	Second disk drive. Used in Disk and Advanced versions of BASIC for input and output.

While cassette filenames can include any characters except colons, hex 00's, or hex FF's, diskette filenames can only use the following characters:

A-Z
0-9
$
@

Video Display Usage - Text Mode

Two different video display adapters are available for use with the IBM PC; the IBM Monochrome Display/Printer Adapter and the Color/Graphics Monitor Adapter.

The IBM Monochrome Display/Printer Adapter allows the user to display **text** in black and white. By text, we mean all of the characters in the regular character set (i.e. letters, numbers, symbols, etc.). The Monochrome Display/Printer Adapter also offers some graphics capability via the special line and block characters.

With the Color/Graphics Monitor Adapter, the user can display text in any one of 16 different colors. Text can still be specified in black and white by specifying these in the SCREEN or COLOR statements.

In the text mode, the screen can be visualized as a matrix consisting of 25 horizontal lines, each with 40 or 80 character positions. The lines are numbered from 1 to 25 from top to bottom. The character positions are numbered from 1 to 40 or 1 to 80 from left to right.

Every text character displayed on the screen in the text mode consists of two parts; the foreground and the background. The foreground is the actual character, while the background is the outline surrounding the character. The foreground and background colors for each character can be set with the COLOR statement. The following colors are available with the Color/Graphics Monitor Adapter:

0 Black	8 Gray
1 Blue	9 Light Blue
2 Green	10 Light Green
3 Cyan	11 Light Cyan
4 Red	12 Light Red
5 Magenta	13 Light Magenta
6 Brown	14 Yellow
7 White	15 High Intensity White

Graphics Mode

The graphics mode is only available if the optional Color/Graphics Monitor Adapter is installed on your IBM PC. Two different resolutions are available in the graphics mode, medium and high resolution. The desired resolution can be chosen with the SCREEN statement.

In medium resolution, the screen is divided into a matrix consisting of 320 points horizontally and 200 points vertically. In the graphics mode, the user has the capability to address any of these points. This capability is known as **all points addressable.**

The points are numbered from left to right and from top to bottom beginning with 0. The beginning point in the upper left hand corner of the screen is assigned (0,0) while the point in the lower right hand corner is assigned (319, 199).

Medium resolution allows the use of four different colors. These are numbered as color 0, 1, 2, and 3. In medium resolution, the user need only select the actual color for color 0. One of two available **palettes** is selected for the other three colors using the COLOR statement. A palette is a group of three colors to be used with color numbers 1, 2, and 3.

Text characters can still be displayed in the graphics mode. The characters will be displayed in the same size as they were in the text mode with a screen size of 25 lines by 40 columns. The foreground will be color number 3, and the background will be color number 0.

In high resolution, there are 640 points horizontally and 200 points vertically. The points are numbered in the same manner as in medium resolution, beginning with (0,0) and ending with (636, 199). In high resolution, only black and white are available, with black being color 0 and white color 1. Text characters can be displayed in high resolution. Eighty characters will be displayed per line, and the foreground (character) will be white with a black background.

Graphics Co-ordinates

The various graphics statements require the specification of the position on the screen where a graphics character is to be displayed. This information is supplied in the form of coordinates given in the form (x,y). x gives the horizontal position and y gives the vertical position. When the coordinates given refer to the actual position on the screen, the coordinates are said to be in **absolute form.**

Coordinates can also be used in **relative form.** In relative form, the last coordinate address referenced is used to determine the new coordinates. This information is supplied in the form of coordinates given in the form (xoffset, yoffset). The values named in xoffset and yoffset indicate the positions to be moved horizontally and vertically from the last point referenced. For example, if the last point referenced was (150, 250) and the xoffset and yoffset were specified as (-10,40), the new coordinate address would be (140, 290).

Chapter 9. BASIC Commands and Statements

Introduction

In this chapter, the commands, functions, and variables used in IBM BASIC are listed with short descriptions. A detailed discussion of each individual command, function, and variable is beyond the scope of this text. However, a more detailed discussion of IBM BASIC is included in another text published by WSI, "BASIC and the IBM PC". This text includes a detailed discussion of each command, function, and variable in IBM BASIC.

Format

The command and its associated arguments will be printed in bold type. All capitalized words are keywords. These may be input in uppercase, lowercase, or both. BASIC automatically converts keywords to uppercase.

Any words, phrases, or letters printed in lowercase italics identify an entry that must be made by the operator. Any items enclosed in brackets [ ] are optional. An ellipsis indicates that an item may be repeated as often as desired. Any punctuation marks must be included where shown.

The following abbreviations may be used.

filespec	refers to a file specification
n-m	refers to line numbers.
filename	refers to a file's name.
x, y	refers to screen coordinates.
z	refers to a number or numeric expression.

BASIC Commands, Statements, and Variables

Command, Statement or Variable	Operation
ABS *(argument)*	Absolute value of *argument.*
ASC *(argument)*	ASC II code for first character of string *argument.*
ATN *(argument)*	Arctangent of *argument.*
AUTO *(n, m)*	Automatic generation of line numbers.
BEEP	Sounds the speaker.
BLOAD *filespec*	Loads a machine language program into memory.
BSAVE *filespec*	Saves a machine language program.
CALL *address (argument)*	Used to call a machine language program.
CDBL *(argument)*	Converts its *argument* to a double precision number.
CHAIN *filespec*	Transfers control to another program given in *filespec* and passes variable to it.
CHR$ *(argument)*	Converts an ASC II code to the corresponding character.
CINT *(argument)*	Converts its *argument* to an integer by rounding.
CIRCLE *(x, y), radius*	Draws a circle with center *(x, y)* and with *radius* specified.

CLEAR [,[*,byte1*] [*,byte2*]]	Sets all numeric variables to zero and string variables to null. Optionally used to set the end of memory and the amount of stack space.
CLOSE [#] *filenumber, ...*	Closes file(s) indicated.
CLS	Clears the screen.
COLOR *foreground background*	Sets *foreground* and *background* colors.
COM *(z)* **ON/OFF/STOP**	Used to enable or disable the trapping of communications acitivity in the device specified by z.
COMMON *variables*	Used to pass *variables* to program being chained.
CONT	Used to continue program execution.
COS *(argument)*	Returns the cosine of its argument.
CSNG *(argument)*	Converts its argument to an integer by rounding.
CRSLIN	Returns the cursor's vertical coordinate.
CVD *(8-byte$)*	Converts its argument (an 8 byte string) to a numeric variable.
CVI *(2-byte$)*	Converts its argument (a 2 byte string) to a numeric variable.
CVS *(4-byte$)*	Converts its argument (a 4 byte string) to a numeric variable.
DATA *constant,...*	Contains numeric and string constants later accessed by Read statements.

DATE$	Used to set or retrieve date.
DEFDBL *variable*	Declares variable type as double precision numeric.
DEF FN	Used to define a string or numeric function.
DEFINT *variable...*	Declares variable type as integer.
DEFSNG *variable...*	Declares variable type as single precision numeric.
DEFSTR *variable...*	Declares variable type as string.
DEFSEG [= *address*]	Used to define current segment of memory.
DEFUSR [*z*] = *address*	Defines the starting address for a machine language subroutine named in z.
DELETE [*n-m*]	Used to delete program lines.
DIM *variable*	Used to declare array variables.
DRAW *string*	Used to draw an object.
EDIT *n*	Used to display a line for editing purposes.
END	Used to stop the program. Closes files and returns to command level.
EOF *(filenumber)*	Used to test for end of file condition.
ERASE *variable*	Used to erase arrays from a program.
ERL	Returns error line number.
ERR	Returns error code.

ERROR *(z)*	Allows user to simulate the error code given or to define his own error code.
EXP *(argument)*	Raises e to the power given in *argument*.
FIELD *filenumber,* z **AS** variable	Defines field in a random file buffer.
FILES *filespec*	Lists files in directory that match file named in *filespec*.
FIX *(argument)*	Truncates *argument* to an integer.
FOR...NEXT [*step*]	Executes a sequence of statements a specified number of times.
GOSUB, *n*	Branches to the specified line number which is included in a subroutine.
GOTO *n*	Branches to the line specified.
HEX$ *argument*	Converts *argument* to a hexadecimal string.
IF *expression* **THEN** *statement* [**ELSE**] *statement*	Executes the *statement(s)* following THEN when *expression* evaluates as true. Otherwise *statement* following ELSE or next program statement is executed.
INKEY$	Reads a character from the keyboard.
INP *(z)*	Reads a byte from the port specified.
INPUT *prompt variable*	Used to read data from the keyboard.
INPUT# *filenumber, variable..,*	Used to read data from the specified file.
INPUT$ *(z, filenumber)*	Used to read *z* characters from the specified file.

INSTR *(z, x$, y$)*	Returns the position where one string appears within another string.
INT *(argument)*	Returns the largest integer less than or equal to its argument.
KEY *z, string*	Allows the function keys to be specified as soft keys.
KEY ON/OFF/STOP	Enables or disables trapping of function or cursor control keys.
KILL *filespec*	Used to erase a diskette file.
LEFT$ *(z, string)*	Returns the leftmost *z* characters in the string specified.
LET *variable = expression*	Assigns the value in *expression* to *variable*.
LINE *(x1, y1) - (x2, y2)*	Used to draw a line or figure on the screen.
LINE INPUT *prompt; variable$*	Used to read an entire line from the keyboard.
LINE INPUT *#filenumber, variable$*	Used to read an entire line from a file.
LIST [*n-m*]	Used to list lines specified on the screen.
LLIST [*n-m*]	Used to list lines specified to the printer.
LOAD *filespec*	Used to load a program file.
LOC *(filenumber)*	Returns the current position within the specified file.
LOCATE *row, column*	Used to position the cursor.

LOF *(filenumber)*	Returns the number of bytes allocated for a file.
LOG *(argument)*	Returns the natural logarithm of its *argument.*
LPOS *(z)*	Returns the position of the print head.
LPRINT [*data*]	Sends data to the printer.
LSET *variable$ = string*	Left justifies a string in a field.
MERGE *filespec*	Used to merge saved program with program in memory.
MID$ *(string, z1, z2)*	Returns *z2* characters from *string* beginning at position *z1*.
MKD$ *(double prec.)*	Converts double precision value to a string.
MKI$ *(integer)*	Converts integer value to string.
MKS$ *(single prec.)*	Converts single precision value to a string.
MOTOR *(z)*	Turns motor on (non-zero) or off (z = 0).
NAME *filespec* **AS** *filename*	Used to rename a diskette file.
NEW	Erases current program and variables.
OCT$ *(argument)*	Returns octal value of its *argument*.
ON COM	Allows trapping of communications activity.
ON ERROR GOTO *n*	Allows error trapping routine.

ON...GOSUB	Transfers control to indicated subroutine.
ON...GOTO	Transfers control to indicated line.
ON KEY *(z)* **GOSUB** *n*	Specifies line number to be branched to when the specified control or function key is pressed.
ON PEN GOSUB *n*	Transfers control to a specified subroutine when the light pen is activated.
ON STRIG *(z)* **GOSUB** *n*	Specifies the line of a subroutine to be branched to if one of the joysticks is pressed.
OPEN *filespec* **FOR** *mode* **AS** *filenumber* **LEN** = *z*	Opens the file specified for input or output with a specified *filenumber*.
OPEN COM*z options* **AS** *filenumber*	Opens a file for communications.
OPTION BASE *z*	Specifies a minimum value for array subscripts.
OUT *port, byte*	Sends specified *byte* to a machine output *port*.
PAINT *(x, y), color 1, color 2*	Used to fill an area on the screen with color.
PEEK *(z)*	Used to read a byte from the memory location specified.
PEN *(z)*	Used to read the light pen.
PLAY *string*	Used to play music.
POINT *(x, y)*	Used to return the color of the specified point.

POKE *address, byte*	Used to write a byte to a specified memory location.
POS *(z)*	Returns the cursor column position.
PRINT *expressions...*	Used to display data on the screen.
PRINT USING *string; expressions*	Used to display string or numeric data in a pre-defined format.
PRINT# *filenumber, expressions*	Writes data to specified file.
PRINT# *filenumber,* **USING** *string; expressions*	Writes data to file specified using format specified.
PRESET *(x, y), color*	Used to draw a point on the screen in the background color.
PSET *(x, y), color*	Used to draw a point on the screen.
PUT *filenumber, z*	Writes a specified record from a random buffer to a random file.
PUT *(x, y) array*	Writes graphics information to the screen.
RANDOMIZE *z*	Resets the random number generator.
READ *variable...*	Reads information from a data table created by DATA statements.
REM *remark*	Used to include remarks in the program.
RENUM *new, old, value*	Used to renumber program lines.
RESET	Used to close all diskette files and reset the system buffer.

RESTORE [z]	Used to reset the DATA statement pointer.
RESUME *n*	Used to continue program execution after execution of an error recovery routine.
RETURN *(n)*	Returns program control from a subroutine.
RIGHT$ *(string, z)*	Returns the z rightmost characters of *string.*
RND *(argument)*	Used to return a random number.
RUN *filespec*	Used to execute a program.
SAVE *filespec*	Used to save a BASIC program on cassette or diskette.
SCREEN *(x, y, z)*	Returns the ASC II code for the character displayed at the specified screen location.
SCREEN *mode, burst, apage, vpage*	Used to set screen mode, color on/off, display page, and active page.
SGN *(argument)*	Returns the sign of its *argument.*
SIN *(argument)*	Returns the sine of the angle given in *argument* which must be in *radians.*
SOUND *frequencies, ticks*	Transmits sounds through the speaker.
SPACE$ *(z)*	Returns a string consisting of the number of blank spaces specified.
SPC *(z)*	Prints the number of spaces specified.
SQR *(argument)*	Returns the square root of the *argument.*

STICK *(z)*	Returns the x or y coordinates of the joysticks.
STOP	Used to stop program execution, print a break message, and return to command level.
STR$ *(argument)*	Returns the string representation of *argument*.
STRIG *(z)*	Returns the status of the joystick button.
STRIG ON/OFF	Enables or disables trapping of joystick buttons.
STRING$ *(z, string)*	The first character of the specified *string* is returned the number of times specified in z.
SWAP *variable, variable*	Exchange values between 2 variables.
SYSTEM	Used to return to DOS from BASIC.
TAB *(z)*	Used to tab to position z in a PRINT or LPRINT statement.
TAN *(argument)*	Returns the tangent of the angle given in *argument*, which must be in radians.
TIME$	Used to set or return the system time.
TROFF	Used to set the trace flag which prints the line number of each statement in the program as it is executed.
TRON	Used to turn off trace flag.
USR z *(argument)*	Calls the machine language subroutine specified.

VAL *(string)*	Returns the numeric value of its string argument.
VARPTR *(variable)*	Returns the address of the *variable* in memory.
VARPTR *(#filenumber)*	Returns the address for the file control block of the file specified.
WAIT *port, mask*	Halts program execution until *port* specified develops specified bit pattern.
WHILE *expression*	Executes a series of statements as long as *expression* evaluates as true.
WIDTH *z*	Used to set output line width.
WRITE *expression...*	Used to display data on the screen.
WRITE# *filenumber, expression*	Used to output data to a file.

Appendix A. ASC II Character Codes

In the following table, the ASC II codes will be given with any associated characters and control characters (for codes 0-31).

If you wish to display these characters, you can do so by issuing the following statement.

PRINT CHR$ (x)

where *x* is the ASC II code of the character being displayed.

ASC II Value*	Character	Control Character
000	(null)	NUL
001	☺	SOH
002	☻	STX
003	♥	ETX
004	♦	EOT
005	♣	ENQ
006	♠	ACK
007	(beep)	BEL
008	(backspace)	BS
009	(tab)	HT
010	(line feed)	LF
011	(home)	VT
012	(form feed)	FF
013	(carriage return)	CR
014	♫	SO
015	☼	SI
016	►	DLE
017	◄	DC1
018	↕	DC2
019	‼	DC3
020	¶	DC4
021	§	NAK
022	▬	SYN
023	↨	ETB
024	↑	CAN
025	↓	EM
026	→	SUB
027	←	ESC
028	(cursor right)	FS
029	(cursor left)	GS
030	(cursor right)	RS
031	(cursor down)	US

*Decimal

ASC II Value	Character
032	(space)
033	!
034	"
035	#
036	$
037	%
038	&
039	'
040	(
041	)
042	*
043	+
044	,
045	-
046	.
047	/
048	0
049	1
050	2
051	3
052	4
053	5
054	6
055	7
056	8
057	9
058	:
059	;
060	<
061	=
062	>
063	?

ASC II Value	Character
064	@
065	A
066	B
067	C
068	D
069	E
070	F
071	G
072	H
073	I
074	J
075	K
076	L
077	M
078	N
079	O
080	P
081	Q
082	R
083	S
084	T
085	U
086	V
087	W
088	X
089	Y
090	Z
091	[
092	\
093	]
094	∧

ASC II Value	Character
095	—
096	’
097	a
098	b
099	c
100	d
101	e
102	f
103	g
104	h
105	i
106	j
107	k
108	l
109	m
110	n
111	o
112	p
113	q
114	r
115	s
116	t
117	u
118	v
119	w
120	x
121	y
122	z
123	{
124	¦
125	}

ASC II Value	Character
126	~
127	⌂
128	Ç
129	ü
130	é
131	â
132	ä
133	à
134	å
135	ç
136	ê
137	ë
138	è
139	ï
140	î
141	ì
142	Ä
143	Å
144	É
145	æ
146	Æ
147	ô
148	ö
149	ò
150	û
151	ù
152	ÿ
153	Ö
154	Ü
155	¢
156	£
157	¥
158	Pts

ASC II Value	Character
159	ƒ
160	á
161	í
162	ó
163	ú
164	ñ
165	Ñ
166	ª
167	º
168	¿
169	⌐
170	¬
171	½
172	¼
173	¡
174	«
175	»
176	░
177	▒
178	▓
179	│
180	┤
181	╡
182	╢
183	╖
184	╕
185	╣
186	║
187	╗
188	╝
189	╜
190	╛
191	┐

ASC II Value	Character
192	└
193	┴
194	┬
195	├
196	─
197	┼
198	╞
199	╟
200	╚
201	╔
202	╩
203	╦
204	╠
205	═
206	╬
207	╧
208	╨
209	╤
210	╥
211	╙
212	╘
213	╒
214	╓
215	╫
216	╪
217	┘
218	┌
219	█
220	▄
221	▌
222	▐
223	▀
224	α

ASC II Value	Character
225	β
226	Γ
227	π
228	Σ
229	σ
230	μ
231	τ
232	Φ
233	θ
234	Ω
235	δ
236	∞
237	Ø
238	∈
239	∩
240	≡
241	±
242	≥
243	≤
244	⌠
245	⌡
246	÷
247	≈
248	°
249	•
250	·
251	√
252	ⁿ
253	²
254	■
255	(blank 'FF')

Appendix B. Extended Code For Use With INKEY$

Certain keys or key combinations cannot be represented with standard ASC II code. These are represented with extended codes. The INKEY$ variable can be used to read such a code from the keyboard into a variable.

If a two character string is returned via INKEY$, the first character of that string should be the null character (00 hex). Generally, the second character can be used to allow determination of the key that was pressed. The ASC II codes for the second character are given in decimal in the following table with their associated keys.

Second Code	Meaning
3	(null character) NUL
15	(shift tab) ⇤
16-25	ALT Q, W, E, R, T, Y, U, I, O, P
30-38	ALT A, S, D, F, G, H, J, K, L
44-50	ALT Z, X, C, V, B, N, M
59-68	Function keys F1 through F10 (when disabled as soft keys)
71	Home
72	Cursor Up
73	Pg Up
75	Cursor Left
77	Cursor Right
79	End
80	Cursor Down
81	Pg Dn
83	Del
84-93	F11-F20 (Uppercase F1 through F10)
94-103	F21-F30 (CTRL F1 through F10)
104-113	F31-F40 (ALT F1 through F10)
114	CTRL Prtsc
115	CTRL Cursor Left (Previous Word)
116	CTRL Cursor Right (Next Word)
117	CTRL End
118	CTRL Pg Dn
119	CTRL Home
120-131	ALT 1, 2, 3, 4, 5, 6, 7, 8, 9. 0. -. =
132	CTRL Pg Up

Appendix C. BASIC Error Messages

The following table gives all of the BASIC error messages along with the related error message number and a description of the error.

Error	Error Message	Description
1	NEXT without FOR	The variable that follows NEXT does not match any preceding FOR statement.
2	Syntax error	The program line contains errors in punctuation or spelling (ex. misspelled reserved word, deleted parentheses, etc.)
3	RETURN without GOSUB	A RETURN statement is found which does not have a corresponding GOSUB.
4	Out of data	A READ statement is encountered where no more data items are available to be read from DATA statements.
5	Illegal function call	A parameter is sent to a system function that is out of range. Examples of the cause of this error include the following: • A negative subscript. • A subscript that is too large. • A call to a USR function when the starting address for that function had not been given. • A negative record number used with GET or PUT. • Trying to list or edit a BASIC program that is protected.

		• An argument for a function or statement that is not legal.
6	Overflow	A number is larger than that allowed by BASIC. If the overflow occurs with an integer, program execution will stop. With non-integers, machine infinity will be returned with the proper sign. If a number is smaller than that allowed by BASIC, an underflow condition will result. A zero will be returned and execution will continue.
7	Out of Memory	This error occurs when the program is too large for available memory, or if a program contains too many FOR loops or GOSUBS.
8.	Undefined line number	A reference is made in the program for a line number that does not exist.
9	Subscript out of range	An array variable contains a subscript that is outside the range that was given in the DIM statement.
10	Duplicate Definition	The same array was defined twice. The following may cause this error: 1. Two DIM statements were included for the same array. 2. A DIM statement is used for an array after a default dimension of 10 had been established previously.

		3. An OPTION BASE statement which sets an unacceptable array size is encountered after an array had already been dimensioned by a DIM statement or by default.
11	Division by zero	Either division by zero was attemped or an attempt was made to raise to a negative power.
12	Illegal direct	An attempt was made to enter a statement in direct mode that can only be entered in indirect.
13	Type mismatch	The data used for a variable does not match that variable's type (ex. numeric data for a string variable).
14	Out of string space	BASIC assigns available free memory to string variables until that memory is depleted. When this occurs, this message will be displayed.
15	String too long	The user attempted to create a string in excess of 255 characters.
16	String formula too complex	The string expression is too long or too complex. Try breaking the expression into smaller, less complex expressions.
17	Can't continue	CONT was used in one of the following situations. • CONT was used to attempt to start a program that had stopped because of an error.

		• CONT was used to attempt to start a program that had been changed during a temporary halt in execution. • CONT was used to attempt to start a program that does not exist.
18	Undefined user function	A function was called before it was defined with DEF FN.
19	No RESUME	The program branched to an error trapping routine without a RESUME statement.
20	RESUME without error	A RESUME statement is encountered before an error trapping routine was executed.
21	Unprintable error	The existing error condition does not have a corresponding error message. This is generally the result of an ERROR statement with an undefined error code.
22	Missing operand	No operand following an operator such as +, *, AND.
23	Line buffer overflow	The user tried to enter a line with too many characters.
24	Device timeout	Information was not received from an input or output device within an allotted length of time.
25	Device Fault	A hardware error flag was returned by an interface adapter.

26	FOR without NEXT	A FOR statement was encountered without a corresponding NEXT.
27	Out of paper	Either the printer has run out of paper or it is not turned on.
29	WHILE without WEND	A WHILE statement was encountered without a corresponding WEND.
30	WEND without WHILE	A WEND statement was encountered without a corresponding WHILE statement.
50	FIELD overflow	The program contains a FIELD statement in which more bytes are allocated for a random file's record length than were specified for that file in its OPEN statement. Another possibility is a situation where the end of the FIELD buffer was reached while a sequential input/output was being performed to a random file (ex. PRINT#, WRITE#, INPUT# etc.).
51	Internal error	Some problem is present internally in BASIC. Call IBM or your IBM dealer with a description of the circumstances under which the error occured.
52	Bad file number	A file number is referenced that is not currently assigned to an open file, or is not within the range of valid file numbers specified during initialization. Another possibility is when an invalid device name is used in a

		file specification or when the filename is invalid.
53	File not found	A file is referenced in a LOAD, KILL, FILES, NAME, or OPEN that does not exist on the diskette on the specified drive.
54	Bad file mode	This error occurs when the PUT or GET statement was used with one of the following: • a sequential file • a closed file • to MERGE a non-ASC II file • to execute an OPEN with a file mode other than input, output, append, or random.
55	File already open	An attempt was made to open a file that had been previously opened for sequential output or an append. This error also occurs when an attempt is made to kill a file that is open.
57	Device I/O error	An error occurred during a device I/O operation. Error recovery is not possible in DOS.
58	File already exists	The filename used with a NAME statement duplicates that of a filename already being used on that diskette.
61	Disk full	The entire diskette space is being used. When this error occurs, all files will be closed.
62	Input past end	This error statement indicates that an end of file error occurred. This is caused by an INPUT# statement being executed for a

		sequential file whose entire data had already been read or for a null file. By using the EOF function, this error can be avoided. Another cause of this error is an attempt to read from a file that had been opened for an append or for output.
63	Bad record number	The record number used in a GET or PUT statement was either zero or was greater than the allowed maximum (32767).
64	Bad filename	An invalid form is used for a filename.
66	Direct statement in file	Any ASC II files loaded by LOAD or CHAIN should only contain statements with line numbers. If a direct statement is encountered in a program file being LOAD'ed or CHAIN'ed, the LOAD or CHAIN will be terminated. A common cause of this error is the inclusion of a line feed character.
67	Too many files	This error is caused by the user attempting to create a new file via SAVE or OPEN when the diskette directory is full, or when the file specification is invalid.
68	Device unavailable	An attempt was made to open a file to a non-existent device. The device may have been disabled or the hardware may not be present.

69	Communications buffer overflow	A communications input statement was executed with the input buffer already full. When this error condition occurs, use the ON ERROR statement to attempt input again. When ensuing inputs are attempted, the error condition will be cleared unless characters are received at a rate faster than the program can process them. In this case, you can try one of the following: 1. Use 1C: option when you start BASIC to increase the size of the communications buffer. 2. Use a hand-shaking routine with the other computer to send a message to tell it to stop sending data so that the receiving computer can empty its buffer. 3. Use a lower baud rate for data transmission and reception.
70	Disk write protect	The user attempted to write to a diskette that was write-protected.
71	Disk not ready	Either a diskette is not in place or the diskette door is open.
72	Disk media error	Generally, this is due to a bad diskette, although the cause can be a hardware related problem. The user should copy any exist- existing data to a new diskette and reformat the bad diskette. If the formatting fails, the diskette is unusable and should be discarded.

73	Advanced feature	This error occurs when a program attempts to use an Advanced BASIC feature when Disk BASIC is being used. Load Advanced BASIC and run the program under it.

Appendix D. DOS Error Messages

In the following table, the DOS error messages will be listed underneath the name of the program or command causing the error. A description of the error appears to the left of the error message.

Program or Command Causing Error and DOS Error Message	Description
CHKDSK Allocation error for file *filename*	An invalid sector number was located in the file allocation table. The file was truncated at the end of the last valid sector encountered.
LINK Attempt to access data outside of segment bounds	Invalid object file.
FORMAT Attempted write-protect violation	The diskette being formatted is write-protected. This prevents formatting. The user will be prompted to insert a new diskette.
DOS Aux I/O error	An input or output error resulted while using the first Asynchronous Communications Adapter.
DOS Bad command or file name	This error can result if the command entered is not a valid internal command. Also, this error results if a file with the filename extension .COM or .EXE and the same filename entered as a command cannot be found on the specified drive.

STARTUP Bad or missing command interpreter	The diskette on drive A does not contain a copy of COMMAND.COM, or an error occurred during the loading of COMMAND.COM. Try a System Reset. If COMMAND.COM still will not load, try recopying that file from a back-up.
DEBUG BF	Bad flag error. An invalid flag code setting was used. Use the correct code in the Register command.
DEBUG BP	Over ten break points were specified for the GO command. Use GO with ten or fewer breakpoints.
DEBUG BR	Bad register. The Register (R) command was used with an invalid register name.
CHKDSK xxxxxxxxxxbytes of disk space freed	The amount of diskette space specified was designated as being allocated while it was not actually being used. This space was made available for use.
COMP Cannot compare file to itself	The two filenames entered reference the same diskette file.
EDLIN Cannot edit .BAK file rename file	.BAK files are assumed to be back-up files, and cannot be edited. If you do wish to edit a .BAK file, you can do so by renaming it with a different filename extension.

LINK Cannot open temporary file	The directory is filled.
COMP Compare error at offset xxxxxxx	The files that are being compared contain different values at the displayed offset (in hex notation) into the file. The two different values are also displayed in hexadecimal.
DISCOMP Compare error(s) on track nn	When diskettes are being compared, one or more locations on the track named contain different data.
DOS Data error reading drive x. Abort, Retry, Ignore?	Reference - Disk error reading drive x.
DOS Data error writing drive x. Abort, Retry, Ignore?	Reference - Disk error reading drive x.
DEBUG DF	Double flag. Different codes were given for one flag. A flag can only be changed once in the register command.
CHKDSK Directory error file: *filename*	The file specified never had any valid sectors allocated to it. It will be deleted from the directory.
DOS Disk boot failure	An error occured during the boot (loading) of DOS into memory.

DOS Disk error reading drive x. Abort, Retry, Ignore?	This error message appears when a disk read or disk write error occurs. A similar error message also appears when a data read or data write error occurs. When one of these messages appears, the system will halt until the operator responds with one of the following. • A - for Abort. The program specifying the read or write operation is ended. • R - for Retry. The read or write operation is attempted again. • I - for Ignore. The system acts as if the error never occurred and continues execution of the program. To recover from the error, the user generally responds as follows: Action 1 - R The operation is attempted again with the hope that the error does not occur again. Action 2 - I The error condition is ignored and the program is continued. Action 3 - A The program is aborted.

	If this error occurs while DEBUG is being executed, the Abort, Retry, Ignore portion of the error message will not be displayed. If you wish to Retry, press F3. If you wish to redisplay the Load or Write command, press Enter.
DOS Disk error writing drive x. Abort, Retry, Ignore?	See preceding.
EDLIN Disk full-file write not completed	This error message appears when an End Edit command was ended because the diskette did not contain enough free space to save the whole file. Any portion of the file being saved that remains in memory will be erased.
FORMAT Disk unsuitable for system disk	A defective track was found on the portion of the diskette where the DOS files were to be written. A diskette with this error can only be used for storing data.
CHKDSK Diskette not initialized	CHKDSK could not identify the diskette's directory or file allocation table. Reformat the diskette. You may be able to copy existing files to another diskette before the reformatting.
DOS Divide overflow	This error is either caused by a logic error resulting in an internal malfunction or an attempt to divide by zero.

LINK Dup record too complex	This error is caused by a problem in the object module created from an assembler source program. You should correct the problem in the source program and rerun LINK.
RENAME Duplicate filename or file not found	An attempt was made to change the name of a file to that of one already existing on the diskette. This error can also be caused when the file to be renamed cannot be located in the specified drive.
DOS End batch job (Y/N)?	This message appears when CTRL-BREAK is pressed while a batch file is being executed under DOS. If a Y is entered, the processing of the batch file will end. If an N is entered, the command that was executing when CTRL-BREAK was pressed will end, and execution of the batch file will continue with the next command.
COMP Enter primary file name or strike the ENTER key to end	The file specification of the first of two files to be compared should be entered.
COMP Enter 2nd file name or drive id.	The file specification of the second of the two files to be compared should be entered. If this filename is the same as that of the first entry (primary filename), just the drive designator need be entered.

EDLIN Entry error	A syntax error is present in the last command entered. This error must be corrected.
COMP EOF mark not found	The end of the data in the last block of the files being compared could not be found. Generally, this message will only occur when comparing non-text files.
DOS Error in EXE file	An error was found in the relocation information placed in the EXE file by LINK.
DEBUG Error in EXE/HEX file	The file included invalid records or invalid characters.
DOS File allocation table bad, drive x. Abort, Retry, Ignore?	See "Disk error reading drive x". If this error continues to occur, the diskette cannot be used and must be reformatted.
DOS File cannot be copied onto itself	An attempt is made to COPY a file and place that file (with the same filename) on the same diskette as the original. Either the name assigned to the copy must be changed, or the copy must be placed on a different diskette.
DOS File creation error	A new filename could not be added to the directory. The CHKDSK program should be run to determine whether the directory was full, or whether this error is due to another cause.
COMP File x empty	Either the first or second file being compared has no data. The empty file is given in x.

COMP File x not found	The file named in x does not exist on the specified drive.
DEBUG DOS File not found	A file specified in a command or command parameter is not present on the indicated drive.
CHKDSK File size error for file *filename*	The file size specified in the directory does not agree with the size allocated for that file.
COMP Files are different sizes	The two files being compared are of different sizes. The compared operation cannot be performed because one file contains data that the other does not.
CHKDSK Files cross-linked: *filename* and *filename*	Both files are assigned the same data block. This error is not automatically corrected. The user must correct the problem himself as follows: • COPY both files. • ERASE both originals. • Check the files for any possible errors.
LINK Fixup offset exceeds field width	A machine language processor instruction references an address continuing a NEAR rather than a FAR attribute. The source program should be edited.
FORMAT Format failure	The diskette should be discarded as a disk error was discovered during the formatting process.
MODE Illegal device name	The printer specified must be LPT1:, LPT2:, or LPT3:.

SYS Incompatible system size	The diskette being copied to contained a copy of DOS that is smaller than that being copied. The system transfer will be aborted. By formatting a blank diskette (with the FORMAT/S command), you may be able to avoid this error by copying files to the new diskette.
DOS Insert disk with batch file and strike any key when ready	During execution of a batch file, the diskette containing the batch file was removed. The processing of the batch file will continue when the user reinserts the diskette and presses a key.
DOS FORMAT Insert DOS diskette in drive x and strike any key when ready	The specified drive does not contain a DOS diskette during an attempted reloading of the command processor by DOS, or an attempted loading of DOS by FORMAT.
DOS Insufficient disk space	The file being written requires more space than that available on the diskette. If you believe that this memory is not valid, run CHKDSK to test the condition of the diskette.
DEBUG, DISKCOMP, DISKCOPY, EDLIN Insufficient memory	The DEBUG, DISKCOMP, DISKCOPY, and EDLIN commands cannot execute as there is not enough available memory.
DEBUG Insufficient space on disk	The diskette to which data is being written does not contain enough available space to hold that data.

DOS Invalid COMMAND. COM in drive x	During the reloading of the command processor, the diskette's copy of COMMAND.COM was discovered to be an invalid version. A valid version of COMMAND.COM must be reinserted. Press any key to continue.
DATE Invalid date	A invalid date was entered or an invalid date delimiter was used. Only the hyphen (-) and the slash (/) can be used as date delimiters.
DOS and Commands Invalid drive specification	An invalid drive specifier was entered in a command or one of its parameters.
LINK Invalid numeric parameter	A numeric value is not given in digits.
LINK Invalid object module	The object module was erroneously formed or was incomplete.
CHKDSK, DISKCOMP, DISKCOPY, FORMAT, SYS Invalid parameter	The parameter entered was not a drive specifier. Be certain that a colon follows the drive letter in the drive specification.
TIME Invalid time	An invalid time was entered or an invalid delimiter was used. A colon must be used as a delimiter between hours and minutes and between minutes and seconds. A period must be used between seconds and hundredths.
LINK Invalid Y/N parameter	The user response to a prompt did not consist of Y, N, or pressing Enter.

EDLIN Line too long	During string replacement, the replacement results in the line extending beyond the 253 character limit. This results in the Replace Text command being aborted.
RENAME Missing filename	The second of the two filenames in RENAME is not given.
SYS No room for system on destination file	DOS cannot be transferred, as the destination file did not contain the necessary reserved space for DOS.
EDLIN No room in directory for file	The diskette specified already has the maximum number of files (64).
DEBUG No room in disk directory	The Write command specified a diskette which already contains the maximum number of files (64).
STARTUP Non-system disk or disk error. Replace and strike any key when ready	A disk read error took place upon system start-up, because the disk directory did not contain an entry for IBMBIO.COM or IBMDOS.COM. Be certain a DOS diskette is being inserted into your drive.
EDLIN Not found	This message is displayed when the string being searched for by the replace or search text commands cannot be located.
DOS Not ready error reading drive x Abort, Retry, Ignore?	Refer to the description for "Disk error reading drive x". Retry is not allowed for this error.

DOS Not ready error writing drive x Abort, Retry, Ignore	Refer to the description for "Disk error reading drive x". Retry is not allowed for this error.
DOS Out of paper	This is caused by the printer not being on or being out of paper.
LINK Out of space on list file	This error is caused when enough disk space does not exist for the List file.
LINK Out of space on run file	This error is caused when enough disk space does not exist for the run file.
LINK Out of space on VM.TMP	This error is caused when there is no more disk space to expand the VM.TMP file.
MODE Printer error	The MODE command was not able to set the printer mode. This may be due to an I/O error, the printer being off, the printer being out of paper, or a not ready (time out) condition.
DOS Printer fault	The printer is off line which prevents it from accepting data.
LINK Program size exceeds capacity of LINK	The load module is too large to be processed.
DOS Program too big to fit in memory	The external command file cannot be loaded as it requires more memory than is available.
LINK Requested stack size exceeds 64K	An entry less than 64K should be made in response to the STACK SIZE: prompt.

DOS Sector not found error reading drive x Abort, Retry, Ignore?	Refers to the description for "Disk error reading drive x". Retry is not allowed for this error.
DOS Sector not found error writing drive x Abort, Retry, Ignore?	Refer to the description for "Disk error reading drive x". Retry is not allowed for this error.
DOS Seek error reading drive x Abort, Retry, Ignore?	Refer to the description for "Disk error reading drive x". Retry is not allowed for this error.
LINK Segment size exceeds 64K	The user tried to combine segments with identical names, which when combined, resulted in a new segment of more than 64K bytes (the maximum allowed).
LINK Symbol defined more than once	Two or more modules were found by LINK that defined a single symbol name.
LINK Symbol table capacity exceeded	The names entered were very lengthy. Use shorter names.
DISKCOPY "Target" diskette unusable	The user is attempting to make a copy on a write protected diskette,
LINK Too many external symbols in one module.	A maximum of 256 external symbols is allowed per module.
LINK Too many groups	A maximum of 256 groups is allowed.

LINK Too many libraries specified	A maximum of 8 libraries is allowed.
LINK Too many public symbols	A maximum of 1024 public symbols is allowed.
LINK Too many segments or classes	A maximum of 256 segments and classes (counted as one) are allowed.
FORMAT Track 0 bad-disk unusable	The boot record, file allocation table, and directory are stored on track 0.
LINK Unexpected end of file on VM.TMP	The diskette containing the VM.TMP file has been removed from the drive.
DISKCOMP Unrecoverable read error on drive x	Six attempts were made to read data on the diskette in the specified drive.
DISKCOPY Unrecoverable read error on "source" disk	Six attempts were made to read data on the diskette on the drive specified as the source drive. The copying will not be finished as DISKCOPY will not be able to continue.
DISKCOPY Unrecoverable verify error on "target" disk	Six attempts were made to verify the write operation on the diskette specified as the target. The copying will not be finished as DISKCOPY will not be able to continue.
LINK Unresolved externals: *symbols*	The *symbols* listed were not defined in the modules or library files specified.

LINK Warning: no stack segment	The user responded with a non-zero entry to the STACK SPACE: prompt when none of the specified object modules contained a statement allocating stack space.
FORMAT Write error	A write error was encountered while the boot record or system files were being written.
DOS Write fault error writing drive x. Abort, Retry, Ignore?	Reference the description for "Disk error reading drive x".
DOS Write protect error writing drive x. Abort, Retry, Ignore?	Reference the description for "Disk error reading drive x".
COMP 10 mismatches aborting compare	The files being compared had 10 mismatched locations. COMP is ended.

INDEX